Gesture of Great Love

Gesture
of
Great Love

Embracing the
Silent Heart of Being *Now*

Tarthang Tulku

Dharma Publishing

Gesture of Great Love
Embracing the Silent Heart of Being *Now*

ISBN 978-0-89800-291-1
Library of Congress Control Number: 2022939968

Printed in the USA by Dharma Mangalam Press, Ratna Ling, 35755 Hauser Bridge Road, Cazadero, CA 95421

10 9 8 7 6 5 4 3 2 1

Dedication

The concepts presented here first emerged some fifty years ago, taking shape as the Time, Space, and Knowledge (TSK) vision. Great love is a natural expression of this vision, a love that encompasses the whole world of past, present, and future beings. As we continue on our journey, may we learn to extend that great love to ourselves; may we touch a deeper field, and come in time to fully embody the meaning of that field of feeling.

I offer my deep gratitude to Jack Petranker, the principal editor, to whom I dictated this book over the course of several months, and Robin Caton, the assistant editor. Several others have assisted me with books over the years, including Abbe Blum, Debby Black, Elizabeth Cook, Hugh Joswick, and Julia Witwer. Great contributions were also made by editors who have since passed on, including Leslie Bradburn, Carolyn Pasternak, and Zara Wallace.

Heartfelt thanks to all who have made a serious study of TSK over the years; many have gone on to be accomplished teachers offering seminars in numerous languages, including Hal Gurish, Piet Hut, Kathleen Jenkins, Ken McKeon, Ron Purser, Elon Goldstein, Ralph Moon, the late Steve Randall, and Steven Tainer. Special thanks are owed to the late Peggy Lippitt, one of the earliest supporters of TSK.

This book is dedicated to the great masters of the Nyingma Lineage; to honored parents; and to the hardworking Western students of the Nyingma mandala— some of whom have labored tirelessly on our Dharma activities for forty or even fifty years. The accumulated merit of these efforts is dedicated to the welfare of all beings; may peace, health, and happiness be embodied in every gesture.

Sending hugs and kisses, extending the greatest love to you all, and infinitely, in all directions, forever.

Contents

Introduction

Our World Today

As I write this book, so many people around the globe are suffering! The COVID-19 pandemic has taken a terrible toll. Children have lost their parents, and parents have lost children, siblings, and friends. Some have become unable to work and their long-term health is threatened; many have nowhere to turn. At the same time, a shocking ground war in Europe is killing civilians and forcing many millions of people to give up their homes, their country, and their way of life. In other places, people are starving, or live in refugee camps with grim prospects for moving on. Out of fear, the police kill people they are supposed to protect, and for the same reason, people use violence against the police. Today, bias is displayed proudly, with ugly images, angry words, and—all too often—violence.

I could go on and on, but I don't have to—you watch the news. The awful things that happen every day are on your screens. They can't be ignored.

And you? How are you faring through all of this?

When a new day dawns, do you start out joyfully, looking forward to what's ahead? As the hours go by, do you welcome the challenges that arise, and the opportunities they represent? When you go to bed at night, are you at peace? Do you feel you used your time well during the day?

I don't mean to put you on the spot, but please reflect: how are you, *really*?

My sense is that most people today are not happy, not balanced, and not at peace with themselves. The world has become increasingly complex, and people everywhere seem barely able to cope. Lonely, hopeless, and frustrated, they swing from one crisis to another, trapped in situations they did not create and do not like. I'm not speaking only of those who are poor, or have health issues, or who lack a decent place to live. Even people who are comfortable, healthy, and privileged spend their lives irritated and depressed.

How heartbreaking this is! And how unnecessary. No matter what the circumstances, everyone can begin the day with appreciation, learn and grow from the challenges that arise, and go to sleep at night at ease, feeling that they have been of benefit to themselves and others. Everyone can shine and share, discover new knowledge, and live a meaningful life.

'Everyone' includes you.

The Root Cause of Suffering

Does this seem like a fantasy, or a Tibetan lama's wild dream? I assure you it is not.

Most people think the root cause of suffering is external: disease, poverty, war, hunger, or misguided political leaders. But it seems to me that the cause of most of our suffering is the mind itself. People in every culture wish to be happy, so what stands in their way? They wish for inner peace, so why are they conflicted and confused?

The mind as it operates now, for almost everyone everywhere, undermines positive goals, saps confidence, and crushes the human spirit. It destroys positive feelings like a repressive dictator. Relying on concepts and language, mind uses words like *right* or *wrong, good* or *bad,* to criticize and judge. It flies from one emotional state to another like a small dust mote in a strong breeze.

I call the operations that support the mind a 'regime.' The regime of mind can be likened to the ministers, administrators, judges, and strongmen who prop up a dictator. Unexamined and unchecked, mind's regime highlights what is negative, emphasizes what is lacking, and ignores the natural 'knowledge-ability' we all have that can put an end to suffering and grant inner peace.

But, however powerful it seems now, the regime of mind is not all there is. Mind can operate differently; it *is* possible to find freedom. You don't have to criticize your-self, blame others, or feel helpless. You can appreciate who you are, *just as you are.* You have a body, a mind, and senses; you perceive, cognize, and feel. This is all you need to create a beautiful, peaceful, and loving inner environment in which to live. You have treasures within you. Please don't forget this!

If you find it difficult to accept what I am saying, here is a way to begin: notice those moments in which you truly experience peace, love, or joy. It doesn't matter how short they are. If you are viewing a sunset, or holding a loved one in your arms, if the stars are out in the night sky, or a bird is singing, and you notice a beautiful feeling, be fully present with that. Touch the feeling deeply and allow it to fill your heart and mind and spill outward, beyond any conceivable borders. Embrace your positive feelings. That is enough to get started.

This may not be the complicated instruction you were expecting, but it is a valuable way to begin. We are not in this world for very long, so it's important to take advantage of every moment. *Now* is the time to discover how to heal, how to open beyond all boundaries to the full richness of human being.

A Different Path

The teachings I share in this book do not directly dupli-cate the wisdom tradition I received as a young man in Tibet. Nor do they require that you adopt a religious outlook. I offer them now because I believe the need for transformation in these difficult times is great. I feel that this kind of presentation can be of benefit to everyone, whether you are a long-time spiritual seeker, or simply a curious person, tired of the way things are.

It is likely that the paths to happiness that you have tried up until now have been based on concepts and ideas, on stories and narrative. For example, if you are self-critical, a voice tells you that you are not good enough, not deserving of happiness. To counter this, you try telling yourself a different story: "I am being too negative!", "I have to stop feeling guilty!" "I am a good person."

But a story is a story, a concept is a concept. Nothing really changes by substituting one for another. Mind quickly reverts to its habitual way of conceptualizing, and soon you are unhappy again.

Speaking in a particular tone, from the biased perspective of 'I', the regime of mind identifies problems and then searches for ways to solve them. Yet, if that were effective, the world's problems would have vanished by now. For in the end, the situations we face so starkly today are the same problems human beings have always faced. That is what makes it so important to try a different approach.

Right here and now, in the middle of fears and worries, surrounded by the complexity of the modern world, you can open to a new way of living. You can let go of the idea that you can't, or you don't know how, or you aren't good enough. You can understand that an anxious, insecure mind will keep looping round and round, identifying problems. There aren't enough solutions in the universe to keep pace with a mind like that! Without avoiding responsibilities, without running away from everyday life, you can be calm and joyful. Instead of living in a world of constant conceptualizing, you can bring ease to body and mind, and simply *be*.

You might think that this way of living is selfish, especially when most of the rest of the world is suffering. But being at peace opens the heart, and an open heart leads to compassion for others. When you are harsh and angry with yourself, you become bitter toward everyone around you. When you learn to embrace yourself, to offer yourself a gesture of love, you become free from limitations and the claims of the ego. Healthy and happy, you have an abundance of inner resources from which to draw.

Hugs and Kisses

As things stand now, the regime of mind sets up a self, the one we name 'I', as its home. It establishes 'I' as real and fixed, with definite characteristics, likes and dislikes, wants and needs, based on past experience. Given this, what choice do you have? It's all set up in advance. If you accept the regime's structure, if you cling to 'your' identity, then the same pattern will repeat over and over again through the course of your life. You will have one set of experiences if your identity is "the one who is quiet and shy" and quite another if you are "the one who is angry and lonely." But, either way, an identity built by the regime is a prison: you are never free simply to be.

That is why a different approach is needed. In our society, hugs and kisses are gestures we use to express connection and love. In this book, I use the words 'hugs' and 'kisses' to express gestures that go far more deeply than wrapping our arms around someone or using our lips to touch theirs.

To hug in the way I mean here, is to let go of all of the structures of mind's regime, including the 'I' that serves as a place of refuge. To truly hug, you have to be homeless, for only then can you embrace whatever arises. When you hug in this sense, you stop insisting on your own position, your own psychology and beliefs. Embracing without reservation, you are free from identity. The heart of your being opens like a clear morning sky.

Hugs touch and enfold. They appear in an instant and then they are gone. Rejecting nothing, they allow for the complete openness of a kiss. And that is vital. For if you cannot kiss, you cannot know the full meaning of love.

Please accept this at a very simple level. When you kiss what you have embraced, that is the lightest of touches, an instant-to-instant transition that offers love and expresses unity. Kisses take you into a world where there is no resistance, no division between subject and object—between the one who kisses and the one who is kissed.

Hugs introduce you to a deep way of connecting, and kisses bring hugs to joyous fulfillment. Together, they transform the ordinary. In the instant of a kiss, senses and concepts come together, with nothing left out. In the middle of any experience, you celebrate whatever arises. You relax into openness with no need for symbols or words.

When you offer a gesture of love, a hug and kiss, you are doing something new, leaving your old 'I' behind. You no longer need to say, "This is that," or, "Now I've got it." You no longer need to ask, "Am I safe?" You open completely—which means also letting go of the notion that there is anything to open.

This is more than saying, "I love you": It is the oneness of being.

Of course, right now you may think you will never be able to do this. When you are used to operating in a certain way, it is difficult to imagine giving it up. But you don't have to. All you need to do is to clear a space for hugs and kisses, wonder and joy, to emerge. Any experience, any thought or sensation, can be a gateway to inner peace.

Time Shapes Our Lives

Our joys and sorrow, our projects and regrets, all unfold in time. Building on the past with its memories, we inhabit the present and turn with fear or anticipation toward the future. Every story we tell, and every event we experience, depends on an understanding of time that unfolds from moment to moment. Time, in our ordinary understanding, manifests experience in ways we cannot control, and its power is absolute. We live in time like a pebble swept along in the current of a river, ignorant of its workings, largely helpless to alter its course.

All this is well known, even undeniable. When we inquire more deeply, however, time starts to seem utterly mysterious. One moment gives way to the next—how does that happen? What links a moment with the moment that just preceded it, or with the moment that will follow? If moments are connected, what separates one from the next? If they are not connected, how can they ever communicate?

We care deeply about the past and look ahead with anxiety or expectation toward the future, but in our ordinary understanding of time, we can never inhabit the past or the future. The present, with its memories and unfulfilled intentions, is all we have access to.

Accepting this model is central to the frustrations and difficulties that make up so much of our lives. The unfolding of time from past to present to future traps us in the structure of cause and effect. Events come *from* a source we may not know and give rise *to* consequences we may not want, and we have no choice but to go along. Because we are so well trained in this particular way of understanding time, we fail to question it.

But must the mechanism of linear time be the whole story? Why do we go along with it when it brings with it so much unhappiness?

Instead of accepting the linear progression of moments as the 'way things have to be', this book offers a deeper understanding of the shape of time. I call this shape, 'the instant'.

Today the words 'instant' and 'moment' are often thought of as synonyms, but I have been told that earlier in the history of English an 'instant' was understood to be outside of time. That is the sense I want to evoke here. We keep a little of this early meaning when we say that something happens instantaneously: in no time at all. You could think of the instant as infinitely small, smaller than the smallest unit of time. Yet because it is outside of time, it encompasses the whole of time. It engages all possible moments of time equally. If past, present, and future are the three times to which we usually have access, you could say that the instant is a fourth time.

In the depth of the instant, suffering may come, but just as suffering in a dream lightens if we know we are dreaming, so the suffering that comes through linear time loses its bite when we understand the instant.

A New Way of Understanding

In the pages that follow, I present several approaches that will help you learn to offer yourself hugs and kisses, dwell in the instant, and embrace the silent heart of being that is your birthright. I encourage you to work with all of them. Please consider them all subjects of contemplation, spaces in which to explore, opportunities for new knowledge, and gateways to transformation.

You do not need to graduate from one approach before moving to another; simply toggle among them, as the chapters in this book do. But please do not judge them. It's best not to reject one approach because it isn't comfortable or stick only with another because you like it best. When you can move among all of these approaches skillfully, knowing which to apply at which moment, you will have the key to a new way of being.

The first approach is the most direct: give yourself hugs and kisses! Love is your birthright. Accept and appreciate, and your appreciation will flower into realization. In truly open moments, you will find clarity. Interpretations will be lighter. Meanings will emerge, but there will be no need to grasp them or make them 'yours'. Nor will you need instructors to tell you what to do.

When you offer yourself hugs and kisses, you respect yourself; you connect with yourself and others. You communicate honestly. At ease in every situation, you can simply *be*.

Right now, the regime of mind may be whispering that you are not ready—that you need to do more, or study more, before you can offer hugs and kisses. Whether this is 'wrong' or 'right' is not the issue. A mind that resists gestures of love needs a special gentleness. So, a second approach presented here is to look honestly at the extent of human suffering—both yours and others—now and throughout history.

You may not want to do this; you may prefer to turn away. I realize that. But I don't offer this approach because I am negative, or because I want to depress you. Quite the contrary. I present it because it is transformative. It touches the heart. It will remind you of where you've come from, and point you to what will come next. It will motivate you to take action—and to take it *now*. Seeing suffering clearly, you can choose differently. You can begin to understand that, far from being selfish, it is the *purpose* of human life to offer gestures of love.

Yet a third approach presented here is active inquiry. By examining the operations of the regime of mind, and closely questioning your assumptions, you learn firsthand how mind has become your enemy instead of your best friend. The regime may be efficient, but no matter what it likes or dislikes, thinks or believes, you are imprisoned by it. If the regime is in control, suffering *will* follow.

You can let that fact depress you, or you can say 'no more'. Using language to explore language, you can touch the depth of not-knowing and begin to taste freedom.

About this Book

Over the past few years, I have had many conversations with Jack Petranker, one of my senior students, on the topics presented here. Jack transcribed our dialogues, and from his transcriptions and other material I passed along to him, he prepared a working manuscript. The manuscript was taken through several additional revisions and brought to completion by another of my senior students, Robin Caton. I have monitored the progress of the various drafts, and reviewed the contents with both editors numerous times.

As you read the chapters that follow, let your body relax and your mind open as widely as possible. It is not useful to struggle to fully understand what I am saying the first time through. Trying too hard only creates tension, and tension prevents understanding. A mind that is tightly wound and committed to its positions, responds only to what it already believes and agrees with. So, it's best to read carefully yet lightly, with an attitude of curiosity. Stop along the way and do the exercises. Experiential knowing, in addition to conceptual knowledge, is necessary to penetrate below the surface of the regime.

Sitting comfortably, eyes gently gazing at the page, relax your body and let the joy of learning fill your heart. When you have finished, you will be a different person—more open, more at ease. It is not hopeless! There is a path . . . a way . . . light.

Then read the book again.

May this volume benefit everyone who encounters it.
May it uplift and comfort all who seek understanding,
all who wish for love, peace, and joy.

Tarthang Tulku
Odiyan, Sonoma County, California
2022

CHAPTER ONE

Our Current Situation

An Honest Look

I feel an obligation to say this at the start so there is no misunderstanding, no pretense that you can keep going on as you have: *No matter who you are or what choices you have made in your life, until you travel a different path, you will inevitably encounter suffering in one of its many forms.*

This is not personal; it is not because you have done something wrong and deserve punishment. Suffering results from misunderstanding, from not knowing the nature of mind and how it operates. We *can* transform ignorance into wisdom, but until we do, suffering in its many forms will manifest. This is simply a truth of the way things are.

Physically, everyone suffers from hunger and thirst, the pain of illness, injury, and abuse. We feel the decline of bodily functions that accompanies aging and increases as we approach the end of life.

Mentally, there is the pain of emotionality, tension, fear, grief, and dis-ease. The modern world is rich for some in material comforts, but poor for everyone in psychological well-being. Anger, resentment, shame, envy, pride, frustration or hatred can cloud the mind for days. So many people spend years feeling lonely, sad, or depressed. They think no one cares about them, and they feel unworthy of love. All of us have inner wounds like these that burst open from time to time. If we pretend not to feel this pain, we pay a price later on: our hearts close down, and we rarely experience joy or ease.

On the global level, there is nowhere to hide from suffering, no place in the modern world where we will not be bombarded by heart-wrenching scenes. A woman flees from war in her homeland with small children at her side; they know no one and have nothing when they arrive in a new country and spend the night freezing outdoors. A young boy whose father has been killed in battle is handed a folded flag by a soldier, part of a ceremony the child is too small to understand. A teenage girl, who has lost both legs to a land mine left from a previous war, struggles to walk again. A homeless man sleeps on a concrete sidewalk in a tattered sleeping bag with only a small piece of cardboard as his pillow.

The depth of the anxiety which people everywhere experience is almost unimaginable—amidst war and disease, hunger, grinding poverty, bias, discrimination, hatred, and much, much more. Today there are new fears: a changing climate that may make much of the earth uninhabitable, and the continuing threat of nuclear war.

It only adds to the sorrow to know that similar suffering has taken place throughout history. In the past few decades, the Tibetan people have suffered greatly, but so have people of different races and ethnicities nearly everywhere on the planet. The World Wars brought annihilation and suffering to millions, and war rages again now. Anger and greed continue to breed hatred and destruction, and the latest sophisticated technology of war in all its forms ensures that conflicts will get deadlier as the decades roll by.

How can we let this continue? The very things that bring us so much joy—the people we love, the earth itself—are suffering. Hasn't this gone on long enough? We need to look at this situation honestly and open our hearts. It is time to stop pretending!

I invite you to reflect on the history of human suffering and to feel it deeply. Begin with your own experience. Exercise 1 can serve as a template for this. It asks you to contemplate your life so far in a detailed and honest way. In some sense this is only a preliminary step, yet it is very important. The more closely you look, the more something stirs within you, the more you begin to wake up to the need for change.

Exercise 1

Reflecting on Life's Stages

Reflect on the stages you have gone through in your life, with a special focus on times of difficulty and negative experiences. The purpose of this exercise is not to dwell on negativity, especially if you carry residues of anger or hurt from the past. It is simply to see that we all, as humans, suffer in similar ways. It is our birthright to be peaceful and happy, so we must find a way to move beyond loneliness, blame, and conflict and live joyously for the benefit of ourselves and others.

Here is the beginning of a template you can adapt to accommodate your own reflections:

> When I was born, I floated in a timeless cloud, crying out to eat when I was hungry and sleeping when I was tired. Later, I lay helpless in my crib, unable to communicate my needs clearly—at times happy and secure, at other times filled with fears and unsatisfied longings.

> Around the age of two or three, I began to be sensitive to the passage of time: I waited restlessly for some promised treat and began to experience what it was like to be bored and restless.

> By the age of six or seven, I waited impatiently for the long hours of the school day to be at an end; I thought restlessly about how long it would be till lunchtime or until my parents picked me up from

some event; I worried about getting homework done on time. When my parents or siblings were anxious or angry, I felt helpless and confused. I wanted to help them but I didn't know what to do. I began to copy their emotions, and I became angry and anxious, too.

By adolescence, I was thinking in longer time periods: the months till I started college, or till summer vacation began. I didn't know who I was or who I wanted to be, so I tried out different clothes, different friends, different interests, hoping something would stick. I fantasized about how it would be in the future, when I was finally grown up—the people I would meet, the places I would travel, the challenges I would successfully overcome, and especially the achievements that others would marvel at. I wanted to be special, better than everyone else. I needed so much praise!

By the time I was ready to leave school, the future had become a greater presence in my life. I saw signs that my parents were aging, and experienced disruptions in my routines. I looked forward to being in control of my own life, but I also felt responsibilities crowd in on me, forcing my life in a direction I was not sure I wanted.

These are just a few examples; you will have your own. Let your feelings as you do this lead you to ask fundamental questions: How much of your energy has been tied up in your own unhappiness? Do you need to continue to live your life this way?

If reflecting back in this detailed way is sobering, right now make a commitment to change. From this moment forward, vow that you will not harm yourself; you will not cause yourself pain; you will not lose yourself in confusion or the terrible force of self-hatred and resentment. Think of this as a silent negotiation with mind. Your demands are simple. You want to find inner peace. You want to live in a wholesome way, rejecting destructive patterns. What you ask of mind is the freedom to do this.

In one way, this contract with mind means making a radical transformation; in another, it changes very little. You can continue living your life as you have been. You can swim in the same river and taste the same waters. But now you will follow different rhythms, different ways. You will not drown in the currents of unhappiness.

Caring Eyes

When you have deeply contemplated the patterns of your own life and made a commitment to self-care, your vision will naturally expand to include the suffering of others. You can say with real conviction, "I am not the only one. My parents, my loved ones and friends, cannot go through a single day without experiencing pain and regret, fear and longing. The same is true of every being all over the world."

Look around you with caring eyes, and you will see the countless ways that people suffer, how they sacrifice their present joy in hope of future happiness. Instead of turning away, trace out these patterns in the lives of those you know. Take your time: let it be real. Then imagine the same patterns at work in every corner of the world, from the beginning of human history.

The next exercise asks you to reflect beyond your personal situation to the suffering that generations of people have endured. Thanks to technology and science, we experience more change in a decade now than other cultures experienced in centuries. In one respect, however, not much has changed. The physical conditions under which we live have improved, but we seem to experience at least as much unhappiness as our ancestors.

To investigate this for yourself, set aside some time to contemplate how people lived in the past. Really feel what it must have been like for them. You can do your own research into world history, or follow along with the timeline below.

EXERCISE 2
Contemplating Human History

Begin all the way back in time, with Australopithecus. This is the first known hominid species; it survived for more than 3 million years on the grasslands of eastern and southern Africa, and likely was able to communicate and plan ahead. Homo habilis, another branch of the hominid tree, is associated with the first sophisticated stone tools and the control of fire. Use your imagination: what were their lives like? What challenges did they encounter? Did they suffer? In what ways?

The origin of language, surely one of humanity's most remarkable leaps forward, is said to have happened between 350,000 and 150,000 years ago. About 50,000 years ago the archeological records show evidence of symbolic behavior, such as music, dance, and art. Let your imagination take you back to those times. What did those early humans or proto-humans feel and fear? How did they make sense of the world?

Agriculture developed in the Fertile Crescent around 12,000 years ago. By about 8,000 BCE, human beings had established permanent settlements; two thousand years later, cities arose, leading to the first true civilizations. According to some accounts, it was then that slavery on a large scale came to be practiced. How fully can you imagine the lives of those slaves, what they felt and how they lived?

Great spiritual leaders lived in the period from the 8th to the 3rd century BCE: Confucius, Lao Tzu, the Buddha, Mahavira, and Zoroaster, followed toward the end of the era by Socrates. Imagine living in a time when all these people walked the earth, a time, perhaps, when transcendent meaning shook hands with everyday reality. But were opportunities for new knowledge available to everyone? What did it feel like to live in those times if you had little access to these great masters or their teachings?

Advances continued as the Common Era dawned. The concept of zero as a number originated in India in the 5th century. The first paper money circulated in the 7th century, and gunpowder, as well as the first printed book, a Buddhist Sutra, dates to the 9th century. Much was changing, yet much remained the same. How was it to live during the plague known as the Black Death, in the 14th century, which killed between a third and half of the population of Europe in just twenty years?

The mass-production printing press, invented in Germany in the middle of the 15th century, worked a silent revolution, promoting literacy for the masses. The 17th and 18th centuries saw the invention of the telescope and microscope. The first half of the 19th century saw the electric motor, followed by a host of inventions that would transform the world: photography, the refrigerator, dynamite, and barbed wire; the telephone, phonograph, and light bulb; the radio, bicycle, and earliest aircraft. Imagine seeing such wonders emerge: how did people cope with a constant flux of new inventions and technologies? Were they happier? Or did their suffering continue?

Learning from the Past

This brief survey is over-simplified, but even at this broad scale history has countless lessons to offer us. Civilizations rose to prominence, then slipped into decay and collapse. Colonizer nations brought death and destruction to the lands they settled, undermining the culture and heritage of indigenous people. Whole peoples suffered enormously, including the Tibetans in the land of my birth who have struggled under Chinese control, doing their best simply to survive. Of course, their suffering is far from unique. I still cannot fully comprehend the fate of the Jewish people during the Second World War: six million killed in service to irrational hatred. There are countless other examples, including whole populations decimated out of the desire of their colonizers to squeeze material wealth from the land. Or populations exposed to diseases for which they had no defense, dying by the tens of millions. Or the millions of human slaves, chained, beaten, and starved, unable to live in freedom, forced to work for the satisfaction and comfort of others.

The pain which we humans experience can never be fully catalogued: from war and disease, insecurity and anxiety, hunger, grinding poverty, treachery, doubt, jealousy, and much, much more.

The pace of inventions will continue to accelerate. We cannot say what new breakthroughs, as yet unimagined, will produce further transformations in human life and human consciousness. Will people suffer in the coming decades as they do today? What will make a difference?

We are all familiar with the voice in mind that says "The problems the world faces are too complicated; I can't change the situation." But what if that voice is only a trick played by mind? Perhaps there is nothing that we lack, nothing we need to struggle to attain. Be ready to appreciate, to offer hugs and kisses to yourself and others, and you will rise from your reflections with renewed energy, keenly aware that you have the potential to do things differently from this moment on.

When you see through the eyes of love, you recognize that everyone struggles; for the most part they live from one experience to the next, believing that each situation that arises is real and lasting. When one mental state ends, they are overwhelmed by the next, with no sense of the transition between them. When you truly see these patterns in action, your heart melts, and you resolve to do your best to lead all beings—starting with yourself—to peace and lasting joy.

CHAPTER TWO

Appreciation and Joy

Joy is Essential

Joy is a natural response to being alive and to the wonders that life presents. As you begin your journey to a new way of being, allow yourself to appreciate each moment you are alive.

If my reference to joy makes you uncomfortable—if a voice in mind tells you that you don't deserve happiness, or that joy is inappropriate while others are suffering—gently allow those whispers to subside. You are following a different approach now, one in which joy is essential. Your well-being depends on a positive foundation, and so does the well-being of others. Enjoying what manifests in the moment is the opposite of selfish: it is a very reliable pathway to love and compassion. In the absence of joy, we feel like we are living in a dark tunnel—tight, anxious and unable fully to breathe. When joy is present, the heart opens and body and breath relax. We feel rich and full, as though we live in a spring meadow with more than enough flowers to share.

If you are not naturally joyful, you can begin to cultivate joy through appreciating the senses. The senses are remarkable treasures. When they are awakened, you can hear an orchestra playing or the sound of wind chimes, see a bird in flight or the sun reflecting off a copper roof, and fully experience the beauty the world has to offer.

Most people don't pay much attention to the senses. They see or hear something only to identify it, or to judge what relationship it has to them: is it useful or worthless, something to avoid or something to want? Having made a judgment, they ignore the sensing part of sensing, where beauty and joy reside.

If you find yourself living in an impoverished world, you may have lost the ability to notice; to see and hear and connect.

Appreciating the Senses

The five senses, plus the mind, are intimately connected with everything that appears in this cosmos. Somehow this planet has manifested, together with the creatures who prowl its surface, glide through its waters, and dart through its skies. There are uncountable things to be seen and the capacity to see them; there are innumerable sounds to hear and the ability to hear them. The nose knows smells, and the body can touch and feel.

Instead of moving instantly to name and judge what is happening, it is possible simply to be present. Even if you do not have access to all of the senses, you can open mind and deeply appreciate whatever arises. For example, some sounds may seem ordinary at first or even unpleasant, but that is just on one level, the level of judgment. You can listen instead to sound as sound, letting whatever you hear become rich and vast. The following exercise can help you. It is especially pleasurable to do this outside.

Exercise 3
Welcoming All Sound

Sit comfortably. Take a few minutes to let go of any tension and bring ease to body and breath. Now, listen; simply listen. Whatever sounds are rising up around you, be with them. If there are quiet moments between sounds, be with them as well. When you find yourself drifting into thoughts or feelings, gently return to listening. That is all you need to do. All sounds are welcome; all come and go. How amazing! Wherever you are, there is a symphony of sound and silence playing for you to enjoy.

As you develop an appreciation for all sounds, you can explore the experience in more depth by noticing even more. For example, when you listen more openly, do areas of tension in your body relax? What happens to your breath as you listen? When sound touches your heart, what do you feel?

The sense of seeing gives rise to different experiences. The eye takes in light, and almost instantly, you recognize color, shape and form. The opportunity for appreciation is there, but a moment later your reactions and judgments usually take over. Can you slow this process down and open to the underlying pleasure of simply seeing?

Exercise 4

Simply Seeing

Sit comfortably, easing body and breath. Let the area around your eyes relax and your gaze soften. Take some time for this. Now look around you; simply see. See shapes, forms, patterns, light and shadow, the nuances of color. You don't need to focus on any particular object, or name anything, or create an inner dialogue about what you are seeing. You can relax and enjoy simply seeing. How intricate and interesting the world is!

You can awaken each of the senses, one by one, tasting their unique flavors. As you appreciate more, your senses will reveal more. This interplay between appreci-ation and new levels of sensing gives rise to a vast field of appearance that has been hidden up until now. The lacy pattern of branches on a bare maple, the small pauses between breaths, the astonishing range of colors on a bird's wing may suddenly present themselves, and you will find yourself living in a new and richer world.

Remembering Joyful Moments

We've all experienced happiness from time to time in our lives, precious moments we carry in our hearts. You can cultivate joy through remembering moments like those, when the clouds of negativity parted and you felt completely joyful. This next exercise can guide you.

EXERCISE 5

Cultivating Joy

Bring to mind a moment when you saw, heard, tasted, smelled or touched something that filled you with delight—a sunrise, a baby smiling for the first time, a small bird chirping in its nest. Contemplate with as much detail as possible, no matter how short the moment may have been. Allow yourself to feel the feelings you felt then, as you re-live the experience.

For example, if you once became deeply involved in a piece of music, let yourself go back to that experience and notice the details. What did it feel like to sit on the seat, feel your feet on the ground, and let the darkness in the concert hall surround you? The musicians began to play and suddenly everything shifted. Maybe it was the melody weaving in and out, or the unexpected harmonies among the different instruments, the elegant leaps, jumps and returns that called to you. Interpretations, self-comments, and reactions subsided, and you became completely immersed in sound. Let those feelings of simple joy expand, moving beyond the boundary of your body and into the space around you.

What was that like? Did your heart open? Were there tears in your eyes at the happiness you recalled?

As you explore the connection between joy, open-heartedness, and presence, you can go beyond even re-living memories. In truth, you don't need a particular occasion, or even a particular set of perceptions, to open your heart. With a little practice, your heart can be open all the time.

EXERCISE 6

Opening the Heart

Make yourself comfortable on your chair or meditation cushion. Let your body become still and your breath become soft and even. Rub your hands together until you feel some warmth. Place one hand on your heart and the other over the first. Feel your heartbeat. That's all, just feel the beating of your heart. Gently invite the warmth from your hands to penetrate your clothing and skin and warm the very center of your heart, relaxing and healing it. Sit awhile, savoring this feeling. Stay with the feeling even after you take your hands away.

Positive feelings are fully available here and now. You can take delight in the wind on your face, the sun on your skin, the sound of birds winging their way over-head. You can accept and appreciate even what seems less appealing: the sound of machinery, the sour taste in your mouth when you wake up, the tightness in your chest that accompanies your worries.

The more you learn to appreciate each moment, see-ing fresh sights, hearing new sounds, the more you will recognize that experience is not composed of fixed and solid entities, that it is better understood as a mirage, no less beautiful for being insubstantial.

A Special Gratitude

Appreciation arises spontaneously when you reflect on all that has made your life possible. Consider the uncount-able number of people and events that have brought you to this present moment: your biological parents; all the people who raised you and served as your teachers; this sheltering earth; the chemicals that came together to create your unique body. Thanks to these causes, and so many others, you have the opportunity now to enjoy all that life presents. You can feel, sense, think and communicate. You can hug life to you, embracing it with an open heart.

The line that separates indifference from appreciation depends on the care with which you reflect. Some of my earliest memories come from when I was two or three years old, not yet weaned. I remember how I fought to be at my mother's breast. I am so grateful to her for her unlimited love; she was ready to sacrifice everything for me. When she disciplined me, her pain was greater than my own.

All of us, no matter what our history, have known kindness. Let yourself look back with special gratitude on the kindness of those who raised you. Perhaps as you grew older, you clashed with them in different ways, but none of that matters for this purpose. When you were tiny and helpless, someone was there to help you learn and grow.

Think also of your parents' parents and the whole lineage of your ancestors. Their lives made possible your life, and that is a debt you can never repay. Reflect on the problems and difficulties they must have faced. You cannot change the past or erase their suffering, but you can offer them your appreciation; you can share with them your joy.

Most importantly, offer appreciation and joy to yourself. When you resolve to care for your body, mind, and spirit, joy flows freely through the depth of your being and transformation becomes possible. Here is a script you can use to start your day, but feel free to use your own words instead.

EXERCISE 7

Committing to Self-Care

As soon as you get up in the morning, take three deep breaths, aware of your inhale and exhale. Let yourself enjoy the way your whole body engages the breath, together with the way that breathing connects you to the world around you.

Then, take a few moments to reflect on your good fortune. Even if you are dealing with obstacles or with sad and painful circumstances, you can remind yourself of how remarkable it is to be alive. You have made contact with teachings that can totally transform your life, and you can choose from this moment forward to live differently. Let this inspire you.

Now, set your intention toward self-care. "Today, and every day, I will care for myself. I will nurture my body, mind and spirit; I will cultivate joy; I will awaken my senses to the riches that are available to me, and share what I learn and know."

You don't actually have to use language. If the intention is there, it is like taking an inner shower that cleanses and refreshes you, opening all your faculties and encouraging your capacity for appreciation.

Offering Joy to Others

Once you begin to enjoy your experience, you can expand joy and offer it mentally to your friends, relatives and loved ones. You can offer joy to the sick and the healthy, to the weak and the strong, to those who live in fear and those who have seized the reins of power. You can share with all beings the possibilities that joy offers, and you can let joy deepen into love. Exercise 8 offers an example of how you might go about this.

EXERCISE 8

Sharing Joy

Whenever you have a joyous feeling, mentally share it with others. You can do this simply, with a wish. It's fine to begin with those you care for.

For example, you might say to yourself, *I feel so happy right now, looking at this sunset; I wish to share this feeling with my parents and children.* Whatever words you use are fine; the important thing is to feel appreciation in the depth of your heart and then share it with others.

When you get very comfortable sharing positive feelings with people you love, you can extend sharing further: *I feel so happy right now, I wish to share this feeling with my parents, my children, my friends; with everyone I know.*

And then further: *I wish to share with all beings who live in my city.* And then—why not?—you can continue on and on: *with those who live in my country, in the world, in the past, the present, and the future,* until you are sharing your happiness with all beings, in all times, everywhere. Yes, even with the bad guys!

When you reflect on all you have, all that you have had, and all there is to come, appreciation will naturally expand. Imagine giving yourself a warm embrace to express your gratitude; imagine a rain of sweet kisses. Really imagine this! Let go of resentment, anger, and painful memories. Welcome all that arises. This present moment, just as it is, is the teacher you have been looking for.

As your life unfolds, you can open each instant fully. There is no need for study or clinging to the right view. Take up the walking stick of joy and set forth on the adventure of the rest of your life.

Interlude

Heart beating,

breath flowing in and out,

body supported by the grace of the earth—

You are here now.

How amazing!

And thoughts?

Let them fly freely through sky-like mind!

CHAPTER THREE

Living Under Mind's Regime

Do your thoughts fly freely? If not, the regime of mind holds you in its grip. It's time to explore what that means.

Body, Language, Mind

To understand why the human journey has been filled with so much suffering, we can frame our inquiry in terms of the three vehicles we have for communicating with ourselves and the world. These are body, language, and mind.

The **body** is the basis for identity: 'I' is the body, and so is the physical body, but 'the body' is also this country we call America, and the world. Whatever serves as the foundation for identity can be thought of as 'body'.

The physical body provides the raw material for our experience. The body can be the source of great joy: the subtle taste of food, the sweet pleasure of fragrance, the intense delight of sex. We find healing in sleep and are stirred by the beauty of art and nature. We appreciate the quality of ease that can course through the senses, and we relish the flow of energy that enlivens the physical body.

Yet the body can also be the source of discomfort. We know well the aches and pains that arise, some of them chronic, some sudden and unexpected—the sting of a bee, a blow to the head, a muscle stretched beyond endurance. The smell of garbage evokes feelings of disgust; not being able to breathe takes over all of experience. When you fall, your whole world crumbles through sudden shock. Exhausted you are helpless and unable to move; overstimulated, you cannot stay still. When you are numb, you stop feeling alive. Hunger and thirst strip the world of all other meaning.

Language turns experience into something that can be labeled and identified. In the act of perception, a special voice comes into play; I call it 'the whisperer'. The whisperer is already active before the senses receive data. It points out everything, explaining and interpreting: "Here is your house; that's a nice car; what are those people doing?"

What is named appears for only a short time and then is gone, perhaps replaced in the next instant by another appearance that is almost identical. Perceptions come and go, rising and falling in waves, rippling outward, echoing, and looping backward and forward.

Mind manifests its own range of experiences. On the positive side, joy transforms sorrows, and bliss opens a whole new world. Caring keeps vision clear. Equanimity insulates mind from bias, while serenity maintains balance. Being at peace is balm for whatever might happen. Courage is a support, and patience makes it possible to act when obstacles arise. Diligence prevents abandoning goals. Acceptance is an ally in every circumstance, while faith and confidence overcome limitations. Respect brings humility, while shame can be a reminder that something has gone astray. Awe opens mind to higher realms, and devotion dissolves the limits that come with putting 'I' at the center.

Mind also supports 'knowledge-ability'. Interest keeps faculties alert, and curiosity is an invitation to journey further. Speculation is an opportunity to know more, and imagination opens worlds of wonder. Mindfulness supports better understanding, and concentration awakens hidden faculties of mind. Discriminating insight is a reliable guide, while wisdom goes beyond the known. Exploration is a valued friend, leading to new insights.

Imprisoned in Ignorance

On the negative side, mind easily manifests toxic qualities. Desire, greed, and longing can never be satisfied.

Possessiveness results in a narrow view of the world. Pride and arrogance distort vision, jealousy brings no rest, and anger distorts the truth. Fear and anxiety create discontent in even the most fortunate of circumstances. Hatred destroys life, and regret and guilt shatter inner peace.

When confusion takes over, mind's natural capacity for knowing yields to dullness or is crippled by ignorance. Concepts and thoughts proliferate, and the world grows small and dark. Doubt destroys certainty; suspicion and paranoia cloud the mind still further. Emotions such as spite and malice, dishonesty, and hypocrisy, are like thieves that rob integrity. Hope and fear prevent clear vision. Indifference may masquerade as equanimity, but it destroys any knowledge of what has value. Laziness undermines goals and causes us to escape into a world where nothing matters.

Whichever way your body, language, and mind engage the world—and these lists could be extended much further—the pattern is the same. The whisperer identifies and you react. Experience unfolds in characteristic rhythms, one mental event succeeding another. Memory provides a link between the present and the past, but the range of the possible remains constant. You experience, you forget, and you experience again. Like a young child suddenly lost on a busy street, you have no sense of how you got to *now*, and no confidence that you can control the future. You accept confusion as the way things are.

Living in Delusion

Letting the mind's regime run unchecked inevitably leads to delusion. By 'delusion' I mean the inability to make sense of what is going on. You cannot see how beginnings link up with endings. You don't know how the 'now experience' arose, to whom it appeared, and so on. Transitions happen unexpectedly, catching you by surprise. Mind is active, but its operations are obscure. It is very much like dreaming: you can never predict the shapes and forms that arise in a dream from moment to moment or understand where they came from. Deluded mind changes on its own, and you cannot say where it will take you next.

Still, you can see the signs of delusion at work. Delusion has a very limited view of what is happening now, so the sense of being limited is a good clue. Another sign is not understanding the consequences of your actions. Looking objectively, you would say that desire leads to attachment and even addiction, and that the consequence is suffering. Living in delusion, however, there is no way to make those connections. You keep drinking too much, you keep buying things you can't afford, you keep distracting yourself with meaningless activities. You just can't see where all of it will lead, and you can't stop yourself.

To live in delusion is enormously frustrating. When obstacles arise, there is no sense of how to respond. You cannot track causes very closely, so you blame others, or you call it 'bad luck'. You may not like what is happening, but you are powerless to do anything about it.

Cutting Through Delusion

It is possible to cut through delusion by strengthening the parts of experience that are fundamentally healthy. You can start by relaxing. For instance, the body has adopted certain habitual gestures and positions. Your shoulders may hunch, your spine may not be straight. You walk in a unique way and that may cause your hips to tighten. Your breathing, too, reflects a characteristic pattern—shallow or deep, fast or slow, depending on stress and worry and the way your thought patterns operate. These are all aspects you can relax. Here is an exercise that can get you started.

EXERCISE 9
Easing into Silence

Begin simply, by sitting quietly and relaxing. You can use any comfortable posture in which your back is straight without being rigid. Let your hands rest lightly on your knees or in your lap, and let your eyes be slightly open, focusing loosely a few feet ahead.

Let go of tension completely so that you are very, very relaxed. Relax your eyes, your forehead, the back of your neck, your hands. As much as you possibly can, let your body become soft, gentle, and loose.

As you do this, your breathing will naturally slow down, becoming even and soft, like a gentle breeze. Lightly notice your inhale and exhale. This is not a strict or formal observing, such as you would use if counting breaths, but a gentle, open awareness that contacts the breath directly and stimulates a quality of evenness within it.

As you sit, loosely and calmly, your thoughts will naturally slow down. You can become aware of the silence within mind. Enjoy any feelings of calmness and spaciousness, and let them expand through body, breath, and mind.

In terms of speech, you can relax your breath, soften your tone and use a gentler voice when you speak. You can choose words more carefully and avoid the harshness of certain expressions. If you tend to blurt out your opinions, you can practice staying silent, and if you have something to contribute, but are usually shy, you can learn to speak up.

Communication depends as much on listening as on speaking. If you don't listen well, if many thoughts run through your mind while others are speaking to you, or you interrupt and don't let the other person finish what they were saying, return to Exercise 3, and practice open listening. You can learn to hear at a deeper level by listening not only to the words someone is saying, but to their tone of voice, to the pattern of sounds and pauses that is their unique vocal signature, and to the feeling tones they are expressing beneath the surface of their words.

As for mind, it changes constantly, but one standard pattern tends to repeat itself: a new situation pops up, and you find yourself inside it, assuming it is real. The whisperer tells you the way things are, and you go along, reacting to what is presented: "I like this and I don't like that." "I feel anxious now, but an hour ago I felt calm."

The way to deal with all this complexity is simply to open and let go. Gently, quietly, you can release your commitment to the pre-established truth of what is happening. The situation will continue to unfold, but it will no longer shape your responses in the same way. Let the body, the breath and the mind be calm. When agitated and emotional thoughts bubble up, you don't need to fight with them or indulge them. If you can relax, and allow the manifestations of mind to come and go freely, you will begin to make a fundamental shift. Here is an exercise to help you with this.

Exercise 10

Thoughts, Like Birds

Sit quietly and relax your body as much as possible. Bring ease to your breath, and let thoughts naturally slow down. Instead of fighting or engaging mental activity, imagine you are visiting a new place where thoughts, sensations, emotions and images are of no concern.

It may help to imagine mind as an empty house with open doors and windows. Breezes drift in and out, now cool and now warm, and thoughts fly about like birds, entering and leaving through the open windows and doors. Some are quiet and calm, some are noisy and demanding. Like an empty house, you can simply be, welcoming all that arises—open, spacious, and accommodating, allowing the flow of experience to arise and fall without comment.

As you relax and allow mind to open like the sky, let go of any thought of what relaxation is. There is no need to adjust or change anything; no need to improve or wonder if you are doing it 'right'. Let even these instructions fly in and out of sky-like mind like a gentle breeze, or a small, lovely bird.

Formal Meditation

If you have a formal meditation practice, you may imagine that this kind of openness will happen automatically if you meditate daily for 20 minutes or an hour. But the situation is more complex than that.

When you start from a sense of 'me' and 'mine', what you discover in meditation is more of the same. The insights that meditation can bring are instantly converted into concepts, variations on positions you already hold. But genuinely new knowledge does not come from confirming your existing likes and dislikes, pros and cons.

Meditation provides access to states of consciousness that are not normally available, so the opportunity is there to conduct a different kind of inquiry, to start in on a new education. Unfortunately, most meditators do not take their meditation far enough. When you sink down below the level of ordinary conscious experience, you may reach a place of peace, but if you stop there, experience remains vague and indefinite. You may feel from time to time that you have gone beyond the regime, but whatever relief you find soon fades, like last night's beautiful dream. The idea that you could unite with mind, make friends with mind, or free yourself from the domain of mind remains more like a fantasy than a real possibility.

The real shift comes when you discover how to refresh and reprogram inner awareness, how to find inner clarity and expand on the clarity already present. All this depends also on appreciation. A distanced or judgmental stance toward your own experience has value, but it will not do the job.

So, ask yourself honestly, is your meditation open and free? Do you marvel at the opportunity you have to enjoy your body and mind and the countless activities going on in every moment? Do you give yourself warm hugs and sweet kisses?

If not, it may be time to approach your practice differently. If you feel that thoughts are a problem during meditation, if you try to control your mind, or if you long to repeat some special, blissful experience you once had, you will only grow anxious. That tension will pervade all your activities, meditation as much as anything else.

Instead, allow for the possibility that meditation has its own rhythm, with times of calm following times of disruption. Just as waves on the surface are not separate from the ocean's depths, the thoughts that ripple on and on are not separate from the depths of silent mind.

Whatever you feel while meditating, let it be. You do not need to change anything or push anything away. Rest in a state where there are no instructions, nothing to do. Whatever is happening does not belong to you, so you do not need to hold on to it or name it. Stay open and you will be kissed by space.

A Different Way of Being

If you do not have a formal meditation practice, or if you have one but it seems to have stalled, then what can you do?

Relax and appreciate whatever is happening, *as it is happening.* Relaxing body, language, and mind, the deeper energies and inner powers of the psyche show up. You get a feel for a different way of being, one that has nothing to do with the regime of mind. It may take time to free yourself fully from mind's patterns, but relaxing is the best way to start.

Relax in the morning when ideas and perceptions begin to crowd in. Relax during the day when the temptation is strong to get caught up in whatever presents itself. Relax in the evening when the day is winding down and you feel the urge to look for distraction.

Here is another exercise you might enjoy.

EXERCISE 11

Newness and Nowness

Go for a walk, or just sit quietly in a place you haven't been to before. Let yourself appreciate the newness, the unknown quality of the space you are in. Anything can happen, or nothing may happen. You don't need to have any expectations or make any plans. Enjoy the newness and the nowness, and allow whatever feelings are present to freely arise. In time, they may ripple outward. Or not.

When calmness is present, there is no need to try too hard to maintain it. If you do, the quality of grasping will keep you tense. Instead of struggling, let body, voice, and mind be open. Let yourself be light and loose, and then relax even further. You will find that compassion and wisdom manifest naturally when you are at ease.

Compassion will take calmness to a deeper level. It will prepare you to offer hugs and kisses to everyone, even those you do not know or do not like.

Peace is Always at Hand

Ease and joy are available in every circumstance. You can meditate in a more formal, structured way if you find it helpful, but if you rely on formal sitting alone for lasting results, you may be waiting a long time. Instead, draw on the inspiration of whatever is happening. You can practice with your thoughts, with your sense impressions, or with whatever manifests. You do not need special experiences, fierce discipline, or formal sitting.

Offer yourself a warm embrace, a nourishing hug, and share your joy with others. It is not complicated. Peace is always at hand. When you touch it, you can share it. That's all.

CHAPTER FOUR

Meet the Gatekeepers

I, Me, Mine, and Mind

Of all the manifestations that proliferate in mind, four—'I', 'me', 'mine', and 'mind'—consistently step forward to shape and control experience. I call them the 'gatekeepers.'

Every human being who has ever lived has an 'I', sometimes called the ego. The most powerful and the most humble among us believe in the 'I' and let it take charge. 'I' needs to feel secure, so it makes itself special, holding itself above and apart from anyone else. 'I' craves respect and fears disgrace, loves success and hates failure. 'I' believes it is the hero of its own story, judging and interpreting according to what things mean to 'me'.

Like any ruler, 'I' clings to its possessions and defends them aggressively. *My* security is paramount; *my* qualities are better and truer than others. *My* family, *my* religion, and *my* country are more important than yours. *My* accomplishments, *my* skills, and *my* desires are the ones that matter. Even *my* suffering, hard as it is to bear, is *mine* and more authentic than yours.

Does this sound familiar?

Then there are all the things 'I' rejects as *not* mine: "It is not my fault that things went wrong." "It was not my mistake; someone else was responsible." "I had no choice." "If you think you've found my weakness, you're wrong."

'I' is the one who wears the costume of doer and knower. When a thought pops up, 'I' announces that 'I' is the one thinking. When something is spoken, 'I' says, "I am speaking."

Mind accepts this meekly, willing in this case to take second place. And who is there to challenge mind?

A Seamless Weaving

I, me, mine, and mind set up the rules and determine what is so. Entities are identified ("That is someone I don't like"), policies are adopted ("I will never apologize") and patterns of thinking and feeling, sensing, and speaking, become lifelong habits. Religion and philosophy, thoughts and feelings, judgments and imagination, personal identity, relationships, possessions: these are all territories controlled by the gatekeepers. In this way, our world is seamlessly woven.

You may already realize that cravings and attachments, disappointments, and confusions, shape your experience. Again and again, you may find yourself settling for petty pleasures and numbing comforts, cheating yourself of the chance to fulfill a larger purpose because you are afraid of challenges or difficulties. The four gatekeepers promote this way of being.

I want to be clear: this is not a theory of human nature, but a description of what is going on. You can test this for yourself by exploring your own experience. If you find you are always worried, constantly planning, a little dull or very restless, you already know how tightly the gatekeepers bind you.

The way to be free is to deepen understanding. Greater knowledge of how mind operates loosens the gatekeepers' hold and allows you to choose a more easeful way of being. For example, the thoughts, feelings, and sensations 'I' claims to own play continuously like a radio. Where do they come from? What space do they occupy? When the instant passes, and a particular thought is gone, where did it go?

These are experiential questions, not theoretical inquiries. To explore them, you need to be aware of what is happening in the instant and look right there, right then.

"Who is thinking?" is not an instruction to speculate, but an invitation to expand awareness now. This is so important! Nothing affects your life as intimately as your understanding—or lack of understanding— of who, or what, is operating mind.

The Basic Question

The most basic question, perhaps, is this: what *is* mind? Tracking the development of the brain doesn't tell us very much about the nature of mind. The brain is there, yes. But how is it we know what red-ness, tired-ness, round-ness are? How does mind label? How does our imagination work, and our creativity?

Scientists don't agree on answers. In fact, it is not easy to say what answers would look like, since answers rely on language, and language makes use of mind's logic and belongs to its regime. Scientists rely on *their* gatekeepers to select questions to research, carry that research out, and reach conclusions. Can we always rely on their judgments? Are there biases at work, or parts of experience being ignored?

We have access to mind, so we need to explore for ourselves.

Still, a similar challenge arises. How can we search our own minds for the truth about mind when words like 'mind' and 'truth' are identified, defined, and verified by the very mind we are searching? This same situation exists even if we challenge mind; if we refuse to accept what mind says is 'true', our rebellion is itself an expression of mind's regime.

So, is all our knowledge nothing but a set-up? Is it all only mind talking to itself?

Whether you quickly answer 'yes' or 'no,' you are still within the regime. Yet accessing a deeper understanding is not that difficult. Let go of the needs and demands of the gatekeepers and see what open awareness has to offer.

Traveling Deeper Within

Let hugs and kisses touch you, and you discover the unity at the heart of being. Space without boundaries carries you beyond the realm of duality, uniting past, present, and future in perfect harmony.

For the mind that believes the gatekeepers' claims of what is so, this may seem impossible. But when you learn to travel more deeply within, you begin to understand that the 'possible' and the 'impossible' are only two labels among many. They have no more basis than any other interpretation mind offers.

EXERCISE 12

Sky Breath

This exercise is especially nice to do outside if the weather permits. Sit comfortably on a cushion or a chair, or you can do this lying down on your back, if you prefer. Relax the body and become aware of your breath, lightly noticing your inhale and exhale.

Now, imagine a beautiful place far away from where you are, with a beautiful, clear blue sky. It might be some place you have been to in the past, or perhaps a place you have always wanted to visit—a beach or a mountaintop, a lakeshore or a meadow. As you bring this place to mind, let each breath come from that distant sky, and each exhale return there, connecting you to that distant, clear blue spaciousness.

That's all. There is nothing else you need to do; simply breathe!

Yes, the gatekeepers are powerful now, operating almost unchecked. But you do not have to fight with them, or deny that they function, for there are countless treasures within their realm. When you stop listening to the whisperer, you realize that you live in a space without borders, in an open house, a clear blue sky. When you really begin to know this, problems and polarities, cause and effect—the very stuff of suffering—lose their hold.

The mind has been trained to like and dislike, desire and push away, so you think that is the only way to live. Educated to be skeptical, you may doubt that great teachers and spiritual friends have demonstrated a different way of being. But even in the West, there have been great thinkers, great artists, poets, and composers, political leaders and deeply spiritual people who have demonstrated a different way of being, who have moved beyond the limitations set by their culture and background.

Let them inspire you. You yourself can manifest a different kind of knowing, like they did, and become a model for others. Hugs and kisses are available, and you can bestow them on yourself and others. If you fail to do this, for what purpose are you living?

Whatever you understand in this moment, you can build on. Everything you need is already here. You can certainly benefit by studying what others have said, but what matters in the end is to investigate your own experience. The gatekeepers are active right now, so why not explore directly? What are the mechanisms they use to support mind's regime? How do they hold you so tightly in their grip?

The next few chapters can help to guide you on your inner journey. But in the end, the path, the tools, the willingness to take the trip, are up to you.

Exercise 13

Beginning a New Story

The beginning of a story is very important; beginnings set the tone for what is to come, and signal to the reader what to expect. 'I' is both the narrator and the hero of the 'story of me.' When 'I' tells the story of your life, how does it begin?

A. Write the first few sentences of a story that begins with the words, "Last year, I . . ." It doesn't matter if what you write is true or not. Write quickly, without stopping to think or edit yourself.

B. Read over what you've written, and now re-write the paragraph as (1) a comedy that will lead to a happy ending; (2) a drama that will lead to a tragic ending; (3) a neutral news story, written by someone who is not involved in the situation and has no stake in the outcome. Again, do it quickly and have fun with it. Can you tell where the stories will end from the shape of the beginnings?

C. Now reflect: when you talk to a friend, how does 'I' usually begin speaking about your life? What is its favorite tone, its preferred genre? Is the story of your life generally a tragedy, a romance, a thriller?

D. The next time you talk to a friend, be aware of how you begin. Instead of speaking from the usual position of 'I,' speak instead as a house with open windows, open doors, and no roof. Let your words be like birds—and see how far they can fly.

CHAPTER FIVE

The Role of Language

A Traitor

Imagine that you are fighting a battle against suffering, an inner battle unfolding in the mind. On your side are insight, compassion, joy, love, caring, and forgiveness. On the side of suffering are greed, hatred, and delusion, jealousy, pride, guilt, blame, and a stubborn clinging to unexamined beliefs. The battle rages, with first one side gaining an advantage, and then the other.

One day, you realize that the suffering side is receiving aid from someone you thought was your ally. When the forces array against you, this traitor insists she is right, ridicules your efforts, and undermines your morale.

Who is it who attacks you this way? When you look closely, you realize with a shock that the traitor is whispering in your own voice. This voice insists that you are not happy; this voice says your problems are real and fixed. You want inner peace, but this voice opposes that goal at every imaginable opportunity. Yet, when you look more closely—you can't find anyone speaking!

If there is only a whispered voice opposing your positive goals, then why are you listening?

The Limits of Language

Often, people who seek happiness rely primarily on language. They say to themselves, "I wish to be free," or "My goal is to find deep comfort, to give myself hugs and kisses." This is fine, and in a limited way assertions like these can be helpful. Self-help books rely on language, and there are many of those on the shelf. But if language is all they offer, beware: language is also what keeps mind's regime in place.

For example, if you announce to yourself the positive insights you have had, language turns them into a possession ('my insights') and this undermines their power. Or, if you criticize yourself for the way mind is working, language instantly generate doubts and confirms a sense of limits. ('I can't do this'.)

How does this happen? When mind engages experience, it teams up with language. It generates names. It assigns identities, speculates, conceptualizes, reacts, and so on—always seeing something more than what is actually there. Someone offers praise, and you puff up with pride, immediately telling yourself stories that go far beyond the simple fact that one person has said something kind. You learn that you have a serious illness, and rather than stay with the basic situation, mind narrates a long, sad story about how life is unfair.

The regime's way of making sense of the world demands additions and exaggerations. Meanings are imposed based on concepts; a whole narrative is built and expanded. You hear about a series of events, and the regime silently composes a history, offering explanations, assigning significance, making judgments about right and wrong. A drama is enacted, all on a hidden, inner stage.

Is/Is Not

At a still more fundamental level, language partners with the regime to set up certain structures. There is knowing, so we believe there must be a knower. Something is communicated, so we believe there must be someone who sends the message and someone who receives it. The regime reaches out to itself and receives feedback. On this basis, we form a sense of our own identity and the world that we inhabit. The regime is both creator and audience, establishing what 'is' and 'is not'.

Here is a simple illustration. Suppose I am working outside. Around me there are trees and water, prayer flags flying, the sound of prayer wheels turning. "That's how it is," I say, because the regime assures me that what I see is 'real'. The point is made and now I can react.

"It's getting cold out," I say, and a further stream of reactions is triggered. Will I be warm enough? I'm sure that by the end of the day I'll be freezing. I wonder whether there will be hot soup at dinner. I wonder who's cooking.

The 'it is' presents the situation. Reasons come up in support of my reactions, and so do surrounding circumstances. From this base and this case, experience arises. I take up the role of actor, owner, and observer, the partner for every new arising. *I know.*

"I know," but wouldn't it be more accurate to say that the regime of mind knows? If I insist that I am the one who knows, how did I get that knowledge? Since *I* is a label applied by language, doesn't it make more sense to say that language knows?

Suppose I pick up the scent of jasmine on the breeze. I say that I am the one who interprets and reacts to that scent, but am I also the one who knows? If I am more precise, it seems that in smelling the jasmine, the nose knows. How?

We can point to the physical receptors, the olfactory nerve, but that level of explanation will not help very much, since now the same questions arise for that nerve. Where does it get its knowing capacity? If we push the process back one step further, to the brain, nothing fundamentally changes. We still don't know how knowing takes place.

For the nose to know, the jasmine that is known must feed back to the knower. Does it 'know' that it must do this?

Instead of being passive, does the jasmine have to actively allow itself to be known? Perhaps it lets itself be known differently to me than to you, or known differently to the deer trotting by, or to the bee that seeks out its pollen. Why must all the knowing come from one side?

EXERCISE 14

Perception, Staged

In a sense, we live in a world perceived. From our limited perspective, it all seems utterly real. But the production and presentation of the real may involve some intricate stagecraft.

Take a short walk. Look around you as you go, imagining that everything you can see is a masterful facade and the hidden, unseen sides of whatever you notice do not, in fact, exist. Try to visualize what you see as the painted scenery of a play, or the hollow structures of a movie set.

Give some attention to the arrangement of these structures in space: their staging. What is presented, what is not presented? What is the shape of the stage? Is there an arch that frames the presentation?

And where are you as you walk? Are you *inside* the scene, an actor on stage? Or are you in the audience, observing? Or are you in both places at once?

Language Traps

In the very act of pointing out what is happening, language sets traps for awareness. Because language demands fixed meanings and solid identities, it shuts down what is truly alive. Words and concepts weave patterns that loop back on each other, creating more confusion. When you grasp the world through labels, you become tied to those labels and the meanings they point out. You are not free.

It is possible to explore in your own experience how this works. First comes contact, as the grasper in mind uses the tool of concepts to reach out and do its grasping. To start, the connection between grasper and grasped may be nothing more than an indefinite feeling, but as content emerges, the contact solidifies. That would be the moment to relax the operation, but if you don't notice it is happening, you don't have the opportunity.

As long as you stay on the level of language, you will be convinced that you know what you are talking about. Secretly, you may feel quite clever. In the end, though, you will be confirming whatever linguistic structure you have already learned to apply. The knowledge that takes form in this way has nothing to do with a deeper understanding. It will not take you beyond concepts—including the concept 'beyond'.

At the same time, you need the right words to act as pointers. That is what is going on in this book. Only when you understand the conceptual meaning of what is pointed out can you get a sense of the direction you want to take. Language may not have a job in a truly new way of knowing, it may fall away entirely, but you need to start by understanding that this is so at the conceptual level.

This does not mean that you are on a grim and joyless quest! Every experience can be approached with care and appreciation. You can cultivate this attitude as you read the next few chapters, which will guide you to explore in greater depth how identity is established, and the problems that arise from ignoring the vibrant dynamic of time.

Exercise 15

Appreciating Inquiry

Here are a few of the many things you can appreciate as you explore and inquire: your eyes that can see the symbols on this page, your mind that can make sense of what is being said as you read this, the light that makes reading possible, the feel of the seat you are sitting on; all the people who have made it possible for you to be reading this today.

Here are some things you can take pleasure in: the feel of this book or your digital reader in your hands, the colors and shapes of the objects around you, the feelings you are feeling no matter what they are; the symphony of sound and silence you can hear whenever you pause to listen; knowledge itself, which brings joy and comfort to body, mind and spirit.

How many items can you add to these lists? Challenge yourself.

Interlude

Can you let go of *trying to know?*

Relax.

Be silent.

Breathe.

Now, walk outside and smile at the sky.

CHAPTER SIX

Establishing Identity

Sameness

When I speak of identity, I am talking about the way the regime of mind turns all that appears into fixed, bounded objects that seem to be real and seem to remain stable through time. The regime's primary tool for identity-making is naming. When the regime of mind labels an appearance, the appearance *becomes* its name: *a rock; a flower; a bird.*

Identity ensures sameness and repetition, and sameness and repetition are the purposes for which identity is established. Mind grasps what is named and identified, and confirms that yes, it is real.

When the identity of an object is established, you your-self, the subject, are caught in the process as well, for you belong to what you identify just as much as it belongs to you. A tree with leaves that are changing color appears, and mind identifies red-ness and yellow-ness and tree-ness, and simultaneously identifies 'you-ness' as the one experiencing the tree. Identity-making establishes the whole structure of you and the object together.

Establishing identity serves the purpose of making you believe that you continue in time and live in a stable world. It permits you to communicate quickly with yourself and others. You can say, "I'd like to buy that ring, please" and watch as the salesperson takes exactly the right object from the jewelry case and puts it in a box. If "ring" had no identity, you would have to say, "I'd like to buy that round shining golden light metal thing that right now is shimmering in the morning light, can you see it?" But then you would also have to use many words to describe 'golden' and 'metal' and 'thing' and 'light' and so on.

And how about 'you'? Would you have enough of a sense of being 'you' to ask for the ring? To communicate, it's efficient for mind to establish identity; it seems to work.

So, why be concerned about identity-making?

Because when we automatically, and *only*, identify through naming, we are ignoring deeper knowledge. And that ignorance leads to suffering.

If you understand only through identity-making, you will limit what you can sense and know. You will see subjects and objects as bounded and separate. You will never know what has not, and cannot, be named. You won't experience the play of light in the open field of appearance, the joyful dance of appearance through time and space.

Instead, you will buy a ring, put it on your finger and for a moment you will be happy that you own something stable and unchanging: *your ring*. You will think your feelings today about the ring will still be your feelings tomorrow.

But you and the ring are *not* bonded. You and the ring are changing fields of appearance. Soon, you, who yesterday wanted the ring, will have different feelings and needs, and the ring that seemed so sparkly and big will appear disappointingly small. Now, you'll be sad and upset. The regime of mind, happy to cheer you up, will whisper, "I know what you need. You need to buy a bigger ring!"

Memory

Memory is the tool mind uses to name and identify. Memory organizes experiences over time; it make sense of your life, as 'sense' is defined by mind. The two work in partnership to establish a world. But how reliable is memory?

For example, do memories exist when the 'I' is not thinking of them? Or do memories have to be created again and again? Does the same memory rise up when mind remembers something, or does mind re-member events differently each time?

Suppose you remember something that happened when you were ten years old. How reliable is that? Are you glimpsing how it was for you then, or are you interpreting it now in the light of all that has happened since then?

How could you know?

EXERCISE 16

Limits of Memory

How many of your thoughts and feelings do you remember? Take some time to consider this and review your experience. Start with the hour before this one. How many thoughts and feelings that took place in that hour do you remember now? Write down the number. Then consider the hour before that and do the same thing: write down the number of thoughts and feelings from two hours ago that you remember now. Keep moving back, hour by hour, until you get to the first hour you were awake today. Then move to the last hour before you went to bed last night and continue moving backwards through time.

When do you stop remembering the thousands of thoughts and feelings you had? Is there an inclination to speculate, or pretend to remember? Of the memories you feel certain of, what makes them stand out? Why do you remember some thoughts and feelings, and not others?

Examining Further

Because it involves language, you might think that identity-making is a conceptual process, and that you can access a deeper and more experiential knowing linked to the senses. However, the senses do not 'simply' sense. Before they even perceive, mind is already labeling, assigning meaning, identifying, and establishing.

Since there is so much at stake in confirming identity, you hold on tightly to the process. You identify the birds flying through the sky and confirm that they are there. In the same way, the sun is there, the mountain is there, the freeway is there. Your lover is there; your friend is there. 'You' and 'mind' are there also, although you would probably admit you don't know where they are, since they have no shape or form.

Appearance and the act of appearing arise together, ready to be identified and established so the appropriate meanings, the meanings established by language, can emerge. It is easy to think that if you understand those meanings, you have understood at a deep level. But, in fact, you have not moved beyond the illusion that words impose. It requires special insight to use language to go beyond language.

Then what can you do? One answer is to find new words or images, new metaphors and poetic forms. But although this might prove fruitful, it requires a level of creativity that not everyone can access. If you are not someone who can, you may find yourself in trouble. The moment 'I' and mind are established at the center of experience, the wrong move has been made. All the rest follows: 'my' and 'me' and 'mind', feelings and judgments, truths that seem real—and the ordinary operation of the senses.

One way to break through this feedback loop is to explore your experience at an even closer level. If mind is not at the center, is there a center at all? Where does mind come from? Where does it go? Who is asking?

These are not questions to consider once and set aside. Each requires careful and repeated contemplation. You need to discover for yourself whether the truths proclaimed by the regime really hold. There is no wrong way, and no right way. There are no worthless experiences. Even the frustration that arises when you contemplate can be the basis for new understanding.

Open the bubble of frustration and what remains? Maybe nothing: no position, no goal.

So there you are—nowhere at all!

Open 'nowhere', too.

Awareness is sharp and clear. You cannot grasp it; you cannot make it your possession. Open awareness and you find—space. You don't need to name it; you are finished with words and labels.

Imagine the silent light of a hundred suns. Now you are getting closer.

<h1 style="text-align:center">Exercise 17</h1>

<h2 style="text-align:center">Light of Understanding</h2>

Sit comfortably and relax the body, letting all tension drain away. Let your breath relax, and mind become deeply silent and open fully, 360 degrees. Imagine mind suffused with a soft, clear light that touches everything, illuminating every dark corner. When anything arises— a perception or image, a thought or feeling—simply bring it together with the clear light of fully open mind.

As you draw nearer to mind's nature, you can trust awakened awareness. And once new knowledge dawns, you can share it with others. This is the greatest gift of all, but also the greatest responsibility.

CHAPTER SEVEN

Seeing with Wise Eyes

The Mirage

Talking about the regime of mind while living within it, it is easy to become confused; new knowledge can float away like blossoms on water. So, pause a bit now and try the following exercise.

Exercise 18

Observing Inner Experience

Sit comfortably, relax the body and breath and without trying for any particular outcome, observe the mind for a few minutes.

When you finish, ask yourself: What was mind doing? Where did you look to observe your mind? *Who* was observing?

You may have noticed image after image, idea after idea, emotion after emotion, popping up like bubbles. You may have noticed endless activity: ruminating, thinking, remembering, describing, interpreting, planning, imagining, speculating, judging, discriminating, wanting, feeling, knowing, narrating, and countless other forms of 'minding'.

At the level of ordinary experience, you accept it all as real and react accordingly. The regime of mind is established, and you take up your assigned role as 'I,' the self, the one who thinks, observes and acts. Then there is more minding, and more.

But the key question, the one the observer forgets to ask is: Who is the one observing?

If 'I' is observing mind, does that mean it is somehow apart from mind, a separate 'thing'?

But, how could that be possible?

If you explore this question with open curiosity, if you are willing to look and trust what you find, you will begin to recognize mind's regime at work. You will discover—perhaps with some shock— that you can't find a 'who' apart from the regime itself. You are sure there is thinking, but you become less and less sure that there is an 'I' who is thinking.

This is when something shifts. Instead of reacting automatically, assuming 'I' is at the center of experience, you slow down and act with a certain detachment. Attuned to the rhythms of appearing, you experience in ways that are less rigid, more open, with more clarity and more compassion.

I hope this has happened for you already; if not, it will. But please don't stop there. As practice and inquiry deepen, there are other levels. Continuing to look with wise eyes, the whole cycle of beginning, middle, and end—cause and effect— begins to seem like a mirage.

Understanding more deeply, you see that mind itself is not an 'entity'; it has no walls, so it has no windows that need to open, and no roof that needs to disappear. Its presentations are already insubstantial as clouds, as dreams, or a rainbow.

Inviting a Different Reality

This may be a difficult point for you to accept because you have been trained to commit yourself to the *realness* of what mind presents. The baby in its crib is constantly taught to assign labels to its experience, and those labels depend on fixed identities. "Here is the ball; this is a cup; put the blue block in the round hole and the red block in the square hole." "*Yes*," mother says, when the baby does what is asked. "*You are right! You are so smart!*"

Continued language-learning reinforces these early lessons. There are nouns, pronouns and adjectives to learn that pin down a world of things and events about which we can feel secure. How could we place ourselves in space without words like into and on, behind or before, up and down? How would we know how to judge without words like pretty, ugly, right or wrong? We label, confirm the reality of what has been named, and react to the label. Body, language, and mind work together to keep the world certain, and maintain the regime of mind firmly in place.

Yet, once we see the constructed nature of this so-called 'reality', we can question the whole structure. The starting point, as always, is appreciation, for without appreciation, we distance ourselves from what we investigate. Distanced, we leave out of the picture our own role as the one who is questioning. It's a little like playing a game of chess. We may solve the challenges the game presents, but that victory does nothing to change our fundamental situation once we have stopped playing.

Appreciation is different. It puts us back in the picture without committing us to what we see. It invites the very different reality of hugs and kisses.

The Value of Analysis

Beginning with appreciation, asking deeper questions, gives us a way to go beneath the many layers of interpretation and reaction. For instance, what is actually involved in *liking* something? What is the experience that underlies the judgment? Is there a place in your body where liking happens? What if you try to expand or condense the feeling of liking? What happens as liking fades away?

What is the point of raising all these questions? We can just go out and offer the world hugs and kisses. Now, everything looks different. Each situation is open, perfectly shining, perfectly light. We do not need to check back to make sure we are acting the right way, because there is no wrong way. We do not need to ask 'why' or 'how' to proceed. It is as though we received a vaccination against negativity, and now we are immune. If something negative does arise, we can open it instantly, since we know it to be a mirage.

There's a lot of appeal to this, but remember: there is a regime, and you are probably still under its sway. If you have a few special experiences, or feel ease, it's easy to convince yourself that you are free, when in fact you have only traded one identity for another. If you truly want to free yourself, truly want to let go, you need to know *who* wants freedom. But that's where the difficulty arises. The regime is not eager for this hidden secret to be discovered.

This is where analysis comes into play. Concepts are limiting, and the answers to your questions will not get you very far. Still, concepts can point beyond themselves. They can challenge the structures we take for granted, and open assumptions to reveal how much we don't actually understand. In the end, we will have to leave concepts behind, but at each step along the way, careful inquiry can prevent a premature sense that we know the nature of reality. If we treat them with care, concepts and language can be valuable guides.

Playing Games

Some people believe that feelings are non-conceptual and inherently more trustworthy than thoughts. But that is misleading. Feelings are still based on causes and conditions. They are no more reliable than anything else in mind's regime. Many kinds of clouds may form in the sky, but they are not the sky itself.

Pleased don't be confused about this. If you are committed to your emotional life, you may find yourself seeking particular feeling-states as a way to relieve suffering. You may be struggling to have special experiences, drinking alcohol, taking drugs, or trying to cultivate a different state of consciousness.

None of that works. It just creates more attachment.

When your approach is goal-centered, you are still measuring your progress. You track the rhythms of experience from the perspective that the regime imposes. You evaluate your understanding: "Is this right or wrong? Do I feel comfortable and at ease, or am I feeling agitated? Is everything okay?" You are still playing games, rejecting parts of experience.

Instead, be completely open, with no walls, no roof, and no floor—and no one having experiences.

EXERCISE 19

Thoughts, Like Clouds

Sit comfortably on a cushion or a chair. Relax the body and let your breath become light and gentle. Sit like a house with no walls, no roof, and no floor, completely open to the air and sky. Breezes drift about, now cool and now warm, and thoughts are as light and as dream-like as clouds. Simply *be*: open, spacious, and accommodating; welcoming all that arises; allowing the flow of experience to enter and depart, rise and fall, without comment.

A Deeply Interesting Journey

Rather than seek experiences that take you into a particular emotional state, let yourself relax into whatever is happening. There is no need to clear things up. Clouds are insubstantial; they come and go. You don't have a blower big enough to blow them away, and even if you did, more clouds would soon form.

Of course, you still need to ask yourself what is valuable to do and what is harmful. At the beginning, you need motivation, so making distinctions makes sense. You say to yourself, "I don't like how acting that way makes me feel," or "When I relax, I feel calmer, and I don't get so

easily confused." In one way, you are fixating on a particular emotional state, or trying to cultivate a particular understanding, but if you are clear on what you are
doing, that kind of fixation will not be harmful.

When you learn how to operate mind, you see that problems or limits arise only because that is how things have
been set up. Since all that appears is like a mirage, there
is no need for antidotes.

You are on a deeply interesting journey, taking you far
beyond what words can express. Along the way, you
may encounter doctrines whose study will bring benefit,
or teachers who offer valuable counsel, but there is no
need to depend only on them. The approach you are
following has nothing to do with yes and no, pro and
con, or with being perfect. What really matters is knowing itself—and this deeper knowing does not depend on
identity.

Interlude

i t i s t i m e n o w t o l e

t g o o f l a n g u a g e a n

d m e a n i n g , o p e n t h

e s p a c e b e t w e e n s y

m b o l s a n d s o u n d , a

n d p l a y i n t h e f i e l

d o f s i l e n t l i g h t .

CHAPTER EIGHT

Mind Magic

Staying a Step Ahead

All of experience is a journey into magic: emotions, sensations, thoughts, and consciousness itself. Magic is the depth of knowing, the meaning of being. The transformation happens as soon as you are ready to offer hugs and kisses.

Can you really embody this way of being and knowing? *Yes!*

The regime of mind sets up structures and points out what is so; it limits and confines. Its way of knowing is to understand the meaning of concepts and language and be able to apply them in any situation. Think back again to the baby learning to talk.

But you can turn your back on all that. When language claims authority, you can reject it. When it leads you in harmful directions, you can turn things around. Anything is possible, because mind's magic show is like a dream, an appearance with no basis.

Magic enters the world when you start to recognize that the appearances that the regime projects are constructed. Yes, sense experiences can catch you, concepts can catch you, the structures of 'I', 'me', and 'mine' can catch you. But when you see the web being woven, you stay a step ahead. You release whatever arises.

In conventional space and time, we know with a conventional knowledge. The mind's regime reacts to the feedback it receives from moment to moment, forming impressions, receiving downloads, pointing out. The regime turns appearances into entities, which seem to come 'from' somewhere and move 'to' somewhere else. The emotional states we constantly fall in and out of are good examples.

All emotionality traces to the gatekeepers and the positions they assume. As soon as the senses are active, the self reaches out to grab something—no matter what it is. The momentum that manifests 'grasper and grasped' is just too strong. It is a kind of addiction: *I* must have *my* convictions and *my* feelings, even if traveling that road leads directly to suffering. You can notice this even as you read this paragraph: the whisperer is agreeing with what is being said or arguing, explaining in its own words or struggling to grasp at meanings.

Above all, the regime likes *answers.*

But suppose there were another way you could journey through life? Things would be very different. The self would not have to stake its claim, set up its territory, or grasp at the next projection. It would not have to make sure that each road connected to the one before. In the end, there would be no need to establish a self, or to journey at all, since whatever is needed would already be there, an endless bounty: a world of silent light.

Words Are Not the Enemy

"I'm not smart enough; I'll never be able to understand this."

The whisperer's voice may be gentle and friendly, but it's still the voice of a tyrant. When you hear it, pay no attention. Whatever it tells you with words and concepts is beside the point.

"Then why all the words in this book?" you ask. That is the whisperer again, insisting that silence is the answer.

Let that go, too. Words are not the enemy. Mind shines and shows, and appearance appears. Concepts shine as well, and words, too, can have hidden depth.

The regime of mind has no choice but to use the tool of identity. But in the open instant, the very qualities that lead to suffering—attachment, grasping, emotionality, confusion—are the seeds of perfect union, with no separation and no territories. Beginning is the same as ending, and one is not different from zero.

Opening matters for this, so do not take it lightly—but do not take it seriously either. Don't make 'open-ness' your latest position; that can only mislead. There is no need to project or fixate. There is no need for concepts, not even the concept "I will not rely on concepts."

If you are still asking how to proceed, I'll say again: it's not complicated. You know this already. Loosen the body and be comfortable. Loosen the breath; let it be free and easy. Loosen the mind; let it relax its constant minding.

'Mind' is a word for something that seems to be real and to exist through time, a house we live in with walls and a roof and a floor, bounded and stable. Let go of that idea. Like all concepts, 'mind' can be opened, too.

When you open in this way, you are not turning over responsibility to a higher power. That would be another way to fixate. Practicing mindfulness would be, too. There are ways to work with mind that focus on particular objects of attention, but this is not one of them.

How the Regime Loses Its Hold

Then how do we escape the regime? We might say that we need to open the meanings that language establishes, but that is misleading, because there is nothing to open and no special state to arrive at.

When the bubble that constitutes a moment of experience appears, the space inside the bubble is the same as the space outside the bubble. When there is no wall, there is no need to find a gate that will let you pass through. You can just relax. The world offers you hugs, and you can offer kisses in return.

Please understand: I am not talking about 'not doing', for 'not doing' is just another concept. You need to be wiser than that. You need to see inside, outside, and in between, before the before, and after the after. 'Nothing' is not a place outside appearance, for outside depends on inside and 'nothing' is not separate from whatever appears.

Systems accompany the regime of mind: mental systems, sense-faculty systems, feeling systems, and meditation systems. But when appearance becomes the play of light, there are no systems. The regime loses its hold.

This does not happen by staying in the center—for if there are no borders, there is no center. It happens when you enter the open field of clear light, where anything at all is free to emerge. This field is more fundamental than the space marked out by 'from' and 'to'. Here, the whisperer falls silent.

Showing and Shining

How often have you said to yourself, "I must concentrate; I must improve?" How often have you said, "I don't know what to do?" You think you are missing something, so you try to follow instructions; if you have none, you make some up.

But it is all so much lighter than that. Instead of trying to understand or analyze, just be the one who is asking. What does it feel like to be the one who feels? Can you expand that feeling and open it up?

Look closely: is there really a distinction between seeing and what is seen, between hearing and the sound you hear?

Look for a place before having and losing, before yes and no. Find the mirror before the image has appeared: the potential to reflect is a kind of shining.

Look for silence, a texture to experience that has the feeling of comfort, cool and balanced. Then relax into being itself. This is not something to possess, not something for 'you' to enjoy. Let go of the thought that "this is happening" and "that is happening." Instead, follow the road that has never been created.

Open completely, so that there are no dimensions left that need to be explored. Live in the Garden of Eden, with abundance everywhere.

You do not need to feel limited by the regime of mind. Hugging and kissing, laughing tears of joy, there is no separation. There never was and there never will be.

Mind moves with remarkable speed. Like the letters for 'hello' written on water, its presentations dissolve instantly. Like clouds in the sky, its constructions never really take form. Obstacles that manifest are not there: they do not *come from* or *go to*. Within experience, there is noticing and sensing, showing, and shining. Rhythms give rise to living experience. Seeing this, you enter a magical realm.

Exercise 20

Field of Light

For events to be experienced, they have to be noticed. But you can open up the recognizable 'character' of experience and make direct contact with the moving clarity that is the open field of light.

Sit quietly, your hands in your lap, your breathing relaxed. When feelings arise, instead of using a label to 'finish' the experience by giving it a name and form (for example, 'anger,' or 'sadness'), stay in the unfinished, open, and continuing space of the feeling, allowing it naturally to expand.

Take time to cultivate the patience and trust that will allow you to give up your assumptions about what is happening. Remember: even 'openness' is open and unfinished, subject to change.

CHAPTER NINE

Offering Hugs and Kisses

An Invitation

As we began many chapters ago, so we repeat: there are so many people who are lost, distracted, lonely, plagued by guilt and wallowing in regret! Are you one of them? Perhaps you long for another, simpler place, where everything is perfect. But even if you could simplify your life in this endlessly complicated world, that is not the solution. The simplest among us still must deal with aging and illness, and we all will one day have to leave our bodies and journey into the unknown.

Can you really accept the many faces of suffering that you experience? If you could give yourself a gesture of love, if you could move beyond illusion, why wouldn't you do that? If you are choosing otherwise, is it because you are afraid, or do you think freedom from suffering is not possible?

These questions are not meant as blame, but as an invitation. Right here and now, you can transform the regime. Just remind yourself not to be trapped by words, even words like 'transform', 'freedom', and 'open'. And beware when you hear a quiet voice whispering, "Yes, I understand. I really get it!" Those soothing words may be lies. If your old problems continue as before, you need to look more closely. Are you seeing with wise eyes? Are you truly beyond?

Pause now and consider. Acknowledge honestly the limits of your current knowledge. To take the most obvious example, no one knows for certain what will happen after they die. In the face of that ignorance, you can find yourself feeling truly humble, for you understand that the knowledge generated by the regime of mind may prove worthless when your time on earth comes to an end.

There is no question of leaving mind behind. Mind itself is doing the looking; the pointer is pointing at the pointer. Still, you do not need to stop there. You can open mind itself. This is not some remote possibility. Whatever appears, you can greet with delight. You can conduct the 'from' and the 'to'.

Cognitive Light

A bubble of thought, or experience, pops up and then is gone. Can you find the inside of the bubble that has already vanished—yesterday's bubble? Can you dwell there?

Before the bubble appears, there must be some kind of potential. You could call it a condition of potentiality. It's already there in each thought and each word. It's more than just the senses operating, but it's before the whisperer. What can you say about that?

Let's look again, even more closely. First an object shows up to one of the senses or to the mind. It doesn't have any shape yet. Now you take the picture; you click the label-button. So that's one side of it. You need the object. I'm not talking only about an object that shows up in front of you; it could also be something you remember or imagine or feel. It doesn't matter.

Now there's the other side: the observer or labeler. For labeling to take place, everything has to be ready. The words are there, and the potential meanings are there, but the labeling hasn't happened yet. You could say that before you can take the picture, you need light. Not physical light: cognitive light. To label what is known, there has to be a knower. *Who is that?*

Consider the rhythms of a river's flow and the water that makes up the river. The two depend on each other. In the same way, waves depend on the ocean, rainbows depend on space, the image depends on eye-consciousness, and reflections depend on the mirror. The mistaken perception of a snake depends on a coiled length of rope, and a mirage in the desert depends on light refracted through heated air.

All these are instants of appearance. How do they arise?

Mind Manifestations

Because we operate at the level of conventional understanding, we must pay heed to how ordinary experience works. The rhythms that shape it may be far removed from what is so, but there is value in exploring them. Each manifestation is different, and we must honor that. On the ordinary level, there is the world of feelings: sad or happy, emotional or calm. Wise eyes see that all such feelings—from ecstatic bliss to soul-numbing despair— are equally conditioned. Yet there they are. Mind itself is simple, unborn, yet its magic generates countless forms.

If you want to be of benefit to yourself and others, think of yourself as the translator between the silent field of light and the endless manifestations that make up our world. When you know both, you can show people a way to negotiate with their own experience, to let go of the regime.

There are ancient teachings that offer ways to do this, but it is not clear that people today can rely on them. Concepts developed in the past to support the kind of inquiry we need may no longer be relevant to our present circumstances. Or perhaps it is simply that we have lost the ability to understand the depth they seek to communicate. Either way, we may need a new way to touch the truth of what is so. That is where we must focus. If you wish to be of benefit, that is your responsibility.

No More Circles

Problems arise within the regime of mind, and human beings have always done their best to solve them. They form relationships and enact laws; they teach morality and celebrate those who show real caring; they support what is just and condemn what is not fair. Yet these solutions fail to hold. Inevitably, they generate new, unanticipated problems. At times human efforts at problem-solving are inspiring, but at other moments in history, the old patterns return and people become deeply discouraged.

We need to find a different way, one with no limits and no need for instructors: a way that simply lets go. We need to offer hugs and kisses, confident that our love and appreciation will touch a level deeper than the neverending stream of difficulties and frustrations.

The regime's way of knowing offers no lasting solution to suffering or to human cruelty and conflict. Why not take that lesson to heart? You can shrug your shoulders and say, "suffering is inevitable, and change is impossible." But you can also challenge yourself to live differently.

What can you do? You can resolve to find a new way of knowing. You can use language against itself. Analyzing mind's operations, you can penetrate the appearances to which conceptual understanding now commits you. You can challenge the senses directly, daring them to become heroes of awakening. You can be ready to play in the field of light and embrace a new way of being.

The real mystery is not somewhere else. It's right here in what we call reality, or truth, or daily life. It's in confusion and loneliness and boredom, and in the thoughts and concepts, and in all the insects and lizards and fruit trees. That's how it all manifests, but before it manifests, before conditions, there is a unity, a play of light.

EXERCISE 21

Play of Light

Whatever is happening, whatever is arising, is a play of light. You are not separate, not an observer: you, too, are light. There are no expectations that anything is going to happen. There is no story of where the light came from or where it is going. There is nothing to observe or fix. Simply be what you already are: open, shining, knowing. A play of silent light.

Treat Yourself Well

Suffering is bad enough. But it is also a sign that you are cheating yourself. If you have the opportunity for joy and inner peace, please don't throw it away. Don't replace your inner treasure with doubts, fears, and unhappiness.

Your first priority is to treat yourself well. You can counter the power of craving, attachment, and addiction by appreciating the good things you have done in your life and the way they made you feel. Stay close to your sense of what has value, and the distractions that pull you away from what you truly care about will not be able to take hold.

There is much beauty in the realm in which we live: sunsets and flowers, bells and birds, our extraordinary oceans filled with countless forms of life that have yet to be identified. There are people, too, who demonstrate every day their courage, their lovingkindness. Think of the hospital workers during the Covid pandemic; think of the paramedics risking their lives during wartime to save victims of bombs and gunfire. Think of neighbors who help neighbors by offering food when a family member passes away, people who rescue homeless animals, who donate food, clothing and money to those who have none. I could list for pages the kindnesses people offer each other every day.

If you cultivate joy and meaning in your life, you move easily into a relaxed way of being. Your spirit is light and open to a pure and luminous energy. Past, present, and future do not catch you up in their momentum, and there is no need to hold on to whatever was the case before. You, too, can be part of the stream of kindness and love, finding your own quiet way to be heroic in the face of the challenges you encounter.

That is why I speak of offering yourself hugs and kisses. Embody your own caring, and you can be aware of feelings, senses, and ideas without being trapped by their content. Appreciation becomes second nature. No longer caught in your own projections, you can delight in how appearances arise and express themselves.

The more you take care of yourself, the more you will find yourself asking how you can share what you know so that others, too, can free themselves from their positions and possessions. As you explore this question, taking it to heart, keep in mind that there are many degrees of ignorance and not knowing, many ways to fall into the numbness of conventional understanding.

Mind's regime undermines all our attempts to break free of our conditioning. It prepares distractions that keep us off-balance, and it fills our heads with illusions. People get caught up in dreams, wishes, and confusion. They stumble around in the same circles, always under the watchful eye of the gatekeepers, always listening with one ear to the ever-present whisperer.

The way to help others who are trapped in this way is to confront the whisperer yourself—to challenge the regime. Before sensory input is processed and the usual messages are downloaded, you can let go. The layers of labels and reactivity simply vanish into silent light: no inside, no outside, no structure.

The depth available in each arising instant is already present. So, right now, in *this instant*, relax fully. Let your heart and senses open. Awakening to a different world, informed by new knowledge, and alive with creative potential, you can *be* a gesture of love. That is the way to benefit beings.

CHAPTER TEN

Time's Dynamic

The Limitations of Identity

As we have seen, one of the central operations of the regime of mind is identity-making. Efficient though it may be, this way of creating a world is inherently divisive and limiting. It simultaneously establishes a subject and an object and presents them as fixed and real.

I, the subject, then take a position toward the object. If I like it, I try to get more of it. If I don't like it, I fight to push it away. If I am indifferent, I lose the opportunity to know it at all. It's as though it was never there.

And, what happens if the 'object' is a thought, feeling, or emotion? I become completely divided from myself. I struggle to feel more of an emotion I like; I fight to push away a feeling that I dislike; and I ignore feelings or thoughts that I have no interest in. If, for example, my identity is tied up in being 'the one who is sad and serious', I may not even realize when joyful feelings arise.

Far from a play of light, I've become a thing of stone.

Time and Change

Identity-making isn't the only way mind's regime undermines the natural joy of being. The regime also distorts the open potential at the heart of time.

Based on what happens, and the choices you make, time becomes another one of your 'problems'. You make a commitment to finish a project in the next week and immediately you feel pressured: you don't have enough time. You make plans for a vacation a month from now and there is too much time to wait. You mark time through rituals—birthdays, graduations, weddings— and then compare yourself now to how you were then: smarter, sillier, thinner, fatter, younger. Then you beat yourself up: "Why didn't I know then what I know now?" Or, "Why didn't I stay as I was then?" How you engage and appreciate time shapes the way you narrate your life.

Past, Present and Future

When you commit to a world of identified things, you also commit to the rhythm of linear time. To say something *is* a chair, means it remains a chair through time, even if that time is brief. That's what 'is' means: lasting through time.

Your own identity is subject to this same linear template. If the thought pops up, "I am bored," the "am" commits you to being bored for at least a certain period of time. The feeling that triggered the label may have come and gone, it may in fact have been an interesting feeling, and not boring at all, but how would you know? The whisperer pronounced, "I am bored," so you must *be* bored until the whisperer says "I am" something else.

Moving from past to present to future, you interpret and speculate, judge and evaluate, claim control or seek favors. The things you like, don't like, or have no interest in, are labelled according to past encounters, present desires, and future hopes and fears. "Am," "is," and "was" lock it all into place. Like a metronome, you repeat—all in the service of 'sameness', of preserving your identity.

Disheartening, isn't it?

Yet however much you cling to your identity, you are also forced to acknowledge how much you have changed. You aren't the same size you were when you were six. You don't have the same thoughts or the same wishes. The things that you did in the past are gone, whether you now label them 'good' or 'bad'. Your feelings shift all the time; the cells in your body keep dying and being reborn. Everything is changing at every level, every instant. Deep down, you know this.

For example, what has seemed most important to you at different times in your life? Were there things you were absolutely sure of when you were younger that you now no longer believe? Things you didn't like that now you do? Did you care deeply about someone once who is no longer important to you? In fact, is there anything that *hasn't* changed since you were young?

If the regime keeps whispering that you and the world are static—that you 'are' and it 'is'— it's telling you a lie you don't have to believe.

Taking Responsibility

One reason you may be clinging to a fixed identity has to do with fear. An unchanging 'you' in an identified world allows you to indulge in the fantasy that you will be here forever. So perhaps you do not *want* to let go.

The fact of impermanence also raises the question of how well you have used your time on earth. Chances are that you have not fulfilled the expectations that your parents and teachers had for you, or met all of the goals you set for yourself when you were young. You may not have transformed your negativities or changed the negative attitudes of others. You may not always have behaved in ways that left you happy with yourself.

Each hour, each minute, is an opportunity, yet most people let the possibilities presented by time slip away. They get distracted or fall into a kind of blankness. They put off doing what they know needs to be done. Emotional and preoccupied, they repeat patterns that have little merit and may be destructive. They accept mind's whisperer, and never challenge what it says.

There is no value to feeling guilty about this. Yet, if you have been letting time slip away, you have been disloyal to yourself for too long.

Going forward you can resolve to use your time meaningfully. It is not that difficult.

Simply commit yourself to what is healthy, vibrant, and positive. You can begin slowly: thirty minutes a day of appreciation and joy; of recognizing what is meaningful to you and not getting distracted; of bringing ease to body, breath, and mind. Then expand: an hour a day, two hours, half a day.

How about the rest of your life?

Examining Time More Closely

Once you are really committed to offering hugs and kisses, you will be motivated to explore the nature of time more closely. Looking inward, you can ask: Is sameness how things actually are? Is time really moving at a steady pace? To feel secure, am I ignoring time's dynamic, with its natural momentum toward freshness and potential? Is the shape of time anything like the face of a clock?

As you do this, you may realize something disturbing. We live in a world of linear time, but the pieces do not quite fit. For example, can we really find the present moment? By the time we finish saying the word 'now,' the present is past.

So, are we ever in the present? Perception takes time to manifest as experience, so maybe we are always in the past, never able to catch up with what is actually happening now.

Or are we always in the present? Are a series of present moments all that there is?

Or, perhaps it's more accurate to say we dwell in the future, since future moments seem to move forward to become the present while we are saying "now."

EXERCISE 22

Time, Unfolding

Sit comfortably and relax your body. Ease into silence. Now, imagine that you are sitting at the exact point where a future moment becomes a present moment, and the present moment becomes a past moment. Do this any way you like. Simply be in the center of time's dynamic, resting there.

What *is* time? How do moments move? What fuels them? Where do they come from, and where do they go?

The whisperer tells you to ignore all this; it's dull and it doesn't matter. After all, your memories line up with the evidence available, the objects you identify are the same ones you have always identified, and you can trace the workings of cause and effect. If past, present, and future are a little hard to get a handle on, that's just how things are. Time passes, there's no doubt about that. And if it isn't clear how it happens, well, that's just part of the fogginess.

The whisperer is leading you astray! There is a great deal more to understand about time and identity, provided you are willing to go beneath the surface. There are the patterns and rhythms of time that seem to ripple outward, fueling your journey through life, moment by moment. There is the question of how tiny units of time connect to each other, so that units of experience appear to flow into each other seamlessly. There is the way experience tightens into repeating loops, each confirmed by its own inner logic.

Establishing Through Linear Time

Whatever is grasped, whatever is established, is constructed by the regime of mind. The regime's processes operate in a linear fashion, relying on the memory of past experience to create and validate the 'real'.

Something appears, and immediately it is identified, using an available label. "That is red." For identification to take place, 'red' must already have been introduced as a possible label at a prior time. 'Red' is cognized now only because it is re-cognized. For appearance and experience to arise, there must be recollection, repetition, echoing. "That is a rose." "This is my friend whom I have known for years."

Each new recognition, each new reaction, confirms the rules in operation. Mind knows that something is real because *it already has decided what counts as real*, and it refers back to 'the real' through a process that requires a notion of linear time. In this way, a sense of 'past-ness' is part of all of our experience.

Because this temporal process is essential to the act of cognition, we accept that appearance is the outcome of a sequence of events. We automatically assume that there is a lineage of previous moments. When we clap our hands—CLAP!—it only takes an instant, but we are firmly committed to the idea that the past is there in the moment of the clap. Something arrives 'from' and something goes 'to'. Each 'now' appears to arise as the result of a previous 'now'.

The regime of mind reacts to the feedback it receives from moment to moment, forming impressions, receiving downloads, pointing out. As it tracks from one point to the next, our experience is not only shaped by the past, but in some sense, also by our expectations of the future.

But can we rely on such expectations? The experience we had yesterday seems similar enough to the experience we have today: the tree outside the window is still there, and we seem to admire it in the same way. So, we expect it to be there in the same way tomorrow. But where is the witness to this sameness? Perhaps yesterday's experience was far removed from today's experience, and today's will be far from tomorrow's.

How would we know?

The Temporal Dynamic

Time appears, space appears, action appears. I appear too, ready to point it all out and react accordingly. My reactions are predictable because they follow the same old routines. Like a washed-up rock band, booking appearances in one club after another, I play the same old standards, again and again.

For me to appear, appearances must appear to me, and they do. Why? Because the space is there for them to appear, the temporal dynamic is there for them to arise, and the knowing is there for them to be cognized. The rhythms of the subject mark out 'my' experience, 'my' mind, 'my' feelings. The rhythms of the object specify the content of experience: the world that presents itself to be known, the interactions that let me react. There are the endless reactions themselves: feeling bored, feeling worried, feeling negative. "I am afraid." "What terrible weather."

Then there are the domains of the inner world, where my personality is crafted. I enact my many identities, and I experience accordingly, confirming the positions I hold and the situations I claim to possess. I belong here and not there; I have faith in this religion, not that one. I work so that I can feel financially secure. I believe in democracy; I practice at my church or temple.

In all these ways I am tethered. I believe and I belong, and my beliefs and my belongings tie me up and tie me down. I hold on tightly, and when something comes up, I react accordingly. I say, "That's it—I believe *that*." If you ask me why, I tell you my reasons, but my reasons are not *it*. I am *in* it, and whatever I cling to—my church, my dogma, my feelings, my mind and my body—are all part of *it*. There is no way I could change it, because it's mine, and I am bound to accept it. There is me, and there is what appears, and there is our interaction.

When you are caught up in time's dynamic, you are constantly bombarded by changing feelings and thoughts you cannot control. Mind itself is simple, yet in its magic it generates countless forms.

Understanding the temporal dynamic that brings it all about, you can let go of the rope that tethers you to the regime of mind and model a new way to be.

Interlude

[ ]

CHAPTER ELEVEN

The Immediacy of the Instant

Regime-Time

The regime lays down the rules that establish the rhythms of linear time, but who taught the regime? Strangely, we never think to ask. The culture we inhabit, or the history we inherit, are possible answers, but culture is an expression of mind, and history is a record of mind's manifestations, so that brings us no closer to a solid foundation.

Time, as presented by the regime, is made up of units. We speak, for example, of moments, minutes, hours, and days; of spring, summer, fall and winter; of beginnings, middles, and ends. Each unit appears to be distinguishable from all other units—this moment is not the last moment or the next moment. And each unit seems to follow from the one that came before in a steady, inexorable march. Once a moment ends, it is gone and the next moment takes its place.

In this way of understanding time, we move forward from the past to an unknown future, and units of time move backward from the future toward us. Each 'future' moment eventually becomes a present moment, and each present moment quickly becomes the past. Before we even finish saying 'now', the present moment is gone. There is only a memory of what was a vital experience; later, even the memory fades.

Meanwhile, we try to grasp each 'now' experience. But even as we reach out to capture one, it's gone. Our internal memory-camera that records the moment gives us at best a static reflection of what we saw, an echo of what we felt. There is a 'pastness' quality to every experience.

At the same time, millions of 'unknown' future moments are hurtling toward us. "Oh no, what will come next?" We have no idea, so we are afraid.

A Paradox

It is important to explore time more closely. If the regime of mind is not presenting a complete picture—if time's structure is more nuanced, more layered than we imagine—then needless suffering is taking place. Understanding time in its fullness can be the key to inner peace and freedom.

We usually imagine that time is like 'beads on a string'. Yet, this metaphor presents us with a paradox.

On the one hand, if time is truly like beads on a string, then how do the beads connect? What is the *string* that ties one moment to the next? Why do the beads only seem to travel in one direction? We experience ourselves and the things around us as continuous and lasting through time, so we must jump from 'bead' to 'bead' somehow. But how? If there is a bridge that allows us to cross from one to another, what could it be made of? Another *kind* of time?

On the other hand, if units of time are not differentiated and separate, and therefore are not like beads on a string, then what is time's shape? We might think time is a continuous flow of present moments, like a river. But if that's the case, then how is it that we can point to past, present, or future, or make sense of cause and effect, or find the origin point of anything?

If all time were 'present' time, ordinary logic tells us that everything would happen at the same time. There would be just one continuous flow of time—infinite, endless— with no way of distinguishing beginnings, middles, or ends.

Units of Suffering

This may all sound very abstract. But keep in mind: there are also units of suffering. For each of the stories that generate suffering, there is a beginning, a point of origin. People cry and feel alone; they feel worthless and consider suicide. What is the history that leads to such sorrows? What is the derivation of such units of experience? There must be original time-points to which the mind has access. If we understood those units, we might understand how feelings and thoughts arise. We might be able to trace the commitment to substance and identity that arises as form appears and takes shape. We might be able to change individual appearances before they arise.

It seems there must be some fundamental unit, or rhythms could not emerge, and experience could not arise. If we knew that unit, we might have a key to understanding the structures that shape our experience.

An Infinitesimal Perspective

The 'instant' is a different model of time. I present it here because it can resolve the paradoxes that a linear model presents and, at the same time, offer a new way to understand experience. It can account for our sense of time's linearity and *also* for its continuity; for how beginnings, middles and ends arise, and *also* for our sense that time flows. The instant considers time from an infinitesimal perspective, not an incremental perspective. While this perspective doesn't entirely accord with our everyday experience, it doesn't undermine it either.

The infinitesimal approach to time posits the 'instant' as the basic unit of time. The 'instant' is the smallest imaginable unit of time there can be without being zero. Bear in mind that we can never actually *identify* a particular instant, because as soon as we do, we can create a smaller unit—for example, half of that instant. So, we accept as an axiom that there *must* be a unit of time that is the smallest one possible, and we call it an 'instant'; at the same time we understand that we can't measure this unit or point to it definitively because once we do, it is no longer the smallest unit possible.

In some sense, we can think of it as similar to a quantum particle. The 'instant' has no set magnitude or duration, but its effects can be known.

By definition, because the instant is always as close to zero—or what we might call 'no time'—as possible, but never arrives there, the instant doesn't move from the future to the present to the past: it remains still, always approaching, but never becoming, the past. The instant bears some resemblance to the symbol we use for zero, since there is only openness at its heart, but it is *not* zero. We might say that, again like a quantum particle, the instant neither 'is' or 'is not'—at least in the usual way we define existence.

The 'instant' can never be captured. It's size and shape can never be determined. Past, present, and future are included within it, all points are generated from it, but there are no units within an instant, so there are no gaps 'between' units that have to be bridged. All time angles are represented in an instant, anything can emerge from it, but there is no linear process, with a beginning, middle, and end.

The Immediacy of the Instant

Our usual way of understanding time breaks time down into moments and then has to find some way of connecting those moments back together. It's an impossible task, because it leaves the flow of time out of account. The instant, however, engages that flow. It restores our link to the dynamic of time. In a sense, it gives us back our lives.

Consider a wave in the ocean. Standing on the ocean shore, we see waves forming, heading in toward land and then collapsing. If we wanted, we could count the number of waves, each separate from the others. That would be something like looking at moments in time.

But all that is based on a fundamental misconception. In truth, there is no such thing as a wave at all. As the water in the ocean moves, driven by the weather and the tides, it takes various forms, and some of those forms are what we call waves. There is no specific 'thing' called a wave, moving through the water; there is just water moving. Looking out over the ocean, we single out the wave as a separate 'thing' but if we went to the place where the wave appears, we would find there was nothing there to mark out as separate—just water in constant motion. That's how it is for the instant also. Not confined to a moment, it is beyond all limits.

Because the ocean is always in motion, forms arise, and we give those forms names: "this wave; that wave." Now we can relate one wave to another; we can analyze and explain and offer accounts. The same holds for the instant. In the ongoing instant, moments arise, and we can link the content of those moments to each other, telling coherent stories of what has happened, is happening, and will happen in the future. In that sense, the instant is temporal, even though it does not happen in time. Yet, dwelling in the instant, we are no longer caught in the content of the stories that unfold from moment to moment. We do not have to take our stand in the truth of what is so, since that truth is simply a moment-by-moment manifestation of the instant.

Growing up, we learn to replace the immediacy of the instant with the linear succession of moments. Our lives take on the shape of a story, with beginnings that play themselves out toward endings, and we learn skills essential to that structure: how to link cause and effect, how to make plans and carry them out. Struggling to make the story conform to our wants and needs, we learn what it means to feel pain and loss, anticipation and regret. Yet all these happenings—the substance of our lives— are about what appears in time, not about time itself.

Linear time as it unwinds from moment to moment tells us what is real, and we go along, bound to the consequences of the temporal order it establishes. Just as a dream has its own logic, so the ordinary world of waking reality has its own logic, constructed out of cause and effect, 'from' and 'to'. It gives us a present moment shaped by the past and future. It keeps us on the surface of time, and it hides from us the depths of the instant.

Yet we can recover the depths of the instant. Without rejecting the realness and logic of the content that time presents, we can release its hold on us, just as we can learn to wake up within the dream.

Not Knowing

Understanding the instant matters, so do not take it lightly—but do not struggle too hard to understand it conceptually either. Don't make the instant another theory you 'believe in', another position, carefully aligned with the other positions you have already taken. That can only mislead.

It's not a question of trying to lift yourself by force out of the ways of knowing time you are familiar with. Just allow for the knowing inherent in what you do not know: a new way of knowing. Let wonder guide you. You can be partners with time. You can find the past in the present and the future in what has already manifested. Language can reveal its own depths, an inner poetry of being.

If the linear structure of time we now accept could not claim its usual unquestioned authority, experience might prove to be more like waves of energy than identified entities. We might grow familiar with the rhythms of arising and passing away. That is why allowing ourselves not to know can have such value. In not knowing, we are already open.

Let certainty be your judge and not-knowing your guide. When you exercise unity-knowledge, you let go of pain and sorrow. You let go of I, me, mine, and mind, notions of linear time, and identity. All of these arise through the regime consulting its map.

Opening Further

How can we draw on the knowledge within not knowing? We have seen already: by opening further, opening fully, opening '360 degrees'.

The mind is always busy with its minding. It wants to know what is related to what; what fits and does not fit. A tension comes with that, a needy quality. *Open up that feeling.*

Relying on sensory perception, we perceive and we react. This thing is good or attractive; that one is bad or disgusting. *Open beyond judging and interpreting.*

The regime analyzes experience. It makes distinctions and then decides. *Open pros and cons; open beyond confusion.*

'Opening' this way may sound worthwhile but be careful. Ordinary 'opening' is not really open. You may make the gesture, or open conceptually, but all the while you leave fixed and in one place the one who opens, or the 'what' of what is opened, or the 'inside' and 'outside', the 'from' and 'to' that you believe opening implies.

Instead, be completely open. You will find that opening is also embracing—that hugs and kisses are the way to silent light.

What a wonderful opportunity! Most human beings have never heard of such possibilities. But now you know: knowledge of the instant is the nectar that can transform all suffering. You can show the world what it needs to heal. You can demonstrate through your conduct that the faculties we possess as human beings contain within themselves peace, compassion, and love.

You can start by appreciating the joy that comes with simply being. When you let appreciation grow in your heart, you will find that things are no longer serious in the same way. You can deal with whatever comes up, effortlessly. Nourish yourself, honor yourself, respect yourself—not in words or ideas, but in your very being, here and now.

CHAPTER TWELVE

Beyond Regime-Time

Presence

How present are you to your own experience? It's a reasonable question to ask. If the way you see the world is based on the labels mind assigns, does that mean that labels come between you and experience, and you are not really present at all?

That is where hugs and kisses come in. Hugs introduce you to experience, and kisses remove all doubts about being present. They offer the union of love. You could even say they lead into the clear realm of *presence*, free from thoughts and concepts, like the pure light of a crystal, shining in all directions.

When you offer kisses to all that arises, there are no conditions or qualifications. Just as there are people you love no matter what they do or who they become, you embrace appearance and let go of interpretation. Image and experience unite, preparing you to see all that appears as insubstantial, like a mirage.

That may sound like something is lost, but just the opposite is true. If appearance has no substance, you can bestow kisses everywhere, throughout space and time. You live in the present-ness of the present. On the surface are the rhythms of past, present, and future, essential to the very possibility of manifestation. But in the depth, presence opens into the immediacy of the instant. Whatever comes up, you are there with it. It is like the prince whose kiss awakens a princess who has been bewitched. All remains soft and gentle.

Now we see things in the light of the regime and linear time, but there is another light, a silent light. That light reveals appearance differently, with no dimensions and no points, no 'to' and no 'from'. In this light, we know the open instant.

An Open Field

Imagine that before the regime of mind constructs experience, there is only an open field, with no beginning and no limits. How long does it take for this openness to give way, to manifest as identified mind?

How can we say, when measured-out time is part of what manifests? The four gatekeepers manifest together as well, each telling the tale of the others. Can we ask who authored that tale? How did it all begin? What set it in motion? How did shadows arise in a world of perfect light?

Imagine a wind arising in empty space. The wind is stirred into being because the senses know how to sense— because the ability is there. In openness, it is different. Nothing has been set in motion, and all possibilities are reflected. Appearances appear as echo, as magical display, as dreams, as rainbows. They manifest but retain their pristine clarity. They need no foundation, and there is no need for an owner.

"But still it happened! How?"

Grasper and grasped are always there. Sound sounds; names get assigned. Is there a beginning to that process? Are there dimensions before dimensions? How can we say? In our ordinary experience, all we know is beginnings and endings, heads and tails: identified units of experience taking form in time and space.

But the instant is available here and now. It neither creates nor destroys, nor does it make judgments. If you can accept that fully and bring it into your own experience, you will learn something new about how manifestation is possible. You can share that knowledge freely with others, connecting heart to heart.

Neither Extreme

The Western-educated mind has a lot of difficulty with this notion. It would rather retreat into concepts. It has so many words to hide behind, so many ways to play the game. Living at this level is like getting lost in a labyrinth, with no way out.

Then what about giving up concepts? This may seem attractive, since the mind freed of concepts is more ready to see, more open to what is always emerging. Still, giving up concepts does not mean that we are free from their hold. The naïve mind has its own limitations. It does not know where to look, nor does it understand how to engage what is seen.

What I am pointing toward here does not fall into either of these extremes. When I say to open, I do not mean that opening is some further step, something *you* have to *do*.

We are here right now, and there is a unit of experience. That unit has a beginning, and also a future. The same is true for every unit, every bubble, for rainbow units and dream units and instant units.

Everything arises and disappears. Think of how many waves there are on the surface of the ocean, and then think how many waves there have been over the past hundred thousand years. At the same time, they are all ocean.

In mind's intricate games, there are boundaries and positions, rules and subtle strategies, like chess on the level of the grandmasters. That is fine for games, but we are not interested in playing games. Instead, let the instant open. You will find a new way to be.

There is a nowness to this newness, unrelated to linear time. You might be tempted to possess it, but when you rest in the clarity of open being, you know that will not work. Possession is the shadow that falls when light is blocked off. Do not settle for that; do not follow the accustomed way.

Instead, take the road that no one has created.

When you embrace all that arises, when you offer gestures of love, subject and object unify. There is no separation; no 'this' and 'that'. You let go of loneliness and guilt. You let go of the gatekeepers, notions of linear time, and identity structures. All of these arise through the operations of the regime; they cannot get a foothold in the shining clarity of the open instant.

Then, what remains?

Hugs and kisses for intrinsic being—silent light and joy.

EXERCISE 23

Welcoming Each New Arising

Identities, sameness and mine-ness have nothing to do with the immediacy of the instant. Sitting with quiet body, settling in completely, you can see this for yourself. In this stillness, there is no need for the mind to wander away into past, present, or future. Let body, mind, and breath be so calm that you are not even present. Welcome each new arising.

You do not need to make something special happen, nor do you have to push anything away. Just lightly focus on the arising instant, and gently expand it. It does not matter whether the instant lasts for a moment, continues for a while, or disappears at once. Touch the possibilities with your imagination and let them expand.

The Special Status of the Instant

When you penetrate appearances, you have access to a deeper way of being, more open and more abundant. You no longer need to seek out guidance or search for security. No one can manipulate you, and whispered stories about fear, worry, guilt, and loneliness cannot touch you. Whatever shows up can be transformed. Or rather, in the immediacy of the instant, there is nothing to transform.

We usually think that each unit of time must have a beginning, a middle, and an end, and that as it ends, it gives way to the next unit. Let go of all that presupposed structure. Just as the instant is not located in any particular place, it is also not located anywhere in regime-time. You can imagine the instant as global, expanding everywhere, with no edges or borders. There is no need to anticipate the next instant or look back on a previous instant, no need to call on memory or imagination.

There are two general approaches to shifting from ordinary linear time, bound up in its stories and patterns—its 'from' and 'to'—to the all-encompassing instant. The first is to see that the presentations of linear time lack foundation. This does not mean they are an illusion. The meal we prepare and enjoy is there, and so is the pain we feel when we lose something or someone we care for. But that 'there-ness' is given by linear time and its temporal order. We can go along with the 'there-ness' without accepting that the 'real' has been established.

The second approach simply goes deeply into what we experience from moment to moment. It finds the depth of the instant directly, shifting attention from the world that concepts and language and labels give us, from stories of cause and effect and an 'I' that experiences. It engages the timeless instant *within* the world of linear time. It discovers the instant in a timing that is smaller than the smallest possible moment, yet more vast than all of time.

Both those approaches are ways of arriving at the instant. And if we arrive at the instant in one moment, we open it everywhere and for all time. Just as space is the same here and a thousand miles away, the instant in this moment is inseparable from the instant two thousand years from now, for in the instant there are no limits or edges, no moments to occupy or contents to identify.

Moments

Moments are the surface of time. We live in such moments, just as we live on the surface of the earth. Experience happens in such moments; without them there would be no experience at all, no separating past from future. But all this is the result of the labels we apply. Just as the sticker on an apple, put there for a computer to scan, is not the apple, so the labels we apply to make experience fit the temporal structure are not the truth of experience.

When we live on the surface of time, suffering is unavoidable, because we accept and reject the content of experience. We say, "This is not how I want it to be," or "This is perfect the way it is; I must be sure not to lose it." But then the next moment comes, and the next, and we can do nothing to stop them and the experiences they bring.

In the depth of the instant, all this is different. Suffering may come, but just as suffering in a dream means little to us if we know we are dreaming, so the suffering that comes through linear time loses its bite. At one level, experience unfolds in linear time, and we react accordingly. At another level, the dynamic of the instant is at work, shaping experience into structure and meaning and making possible transitions from one experience to the next.

How different this is from the way our culture understands time! Because we start from a position of objectivity, of drawing back, most of us seldom reflect on how knowing and appreciation are interwoven. We confirm a specific way of being in time, in which the present moment is defined by the past and the next moment is defined by the present. Instead of exploring the time-less instant, we stay on the surface and never probe too deeply into how feedback from the world around us is possible, or how object and subject communicate with one another, or how awareness is able to be aware. If such questions come up, we have no good way to explore them.

Knowing the instant offers a path. Living in the immediate instant has the potential to change the relationship between knower and known, to open the world for warm, embracing hugs and showers of kisses.

A World without Limits

The instant is not a point that can be pointed out, and time itself is not what we imagine—it is not about activity and happenings. Unknown rhythms are at work, resting in a unity where 'was', 'will be' and 'is' arise together. The instant is a symbol of a world without limits or edges.

At the level of ordinary experience, the linear logic of time's arising seems inescapable. The arrow leaves the bow and hits its target; the sun sets and the moon appears over the horizon. But how does that sequence arise? First, all is quiet in the mind; then a thought appears. Did it trace a path to get here, or did it just pop up? We say, "It must have come from somewhere."

But what is the basis for claiming that?

"Done is done," you might say. "It happened. Now it's over." But how can you confirm the truth of "happened?" Yes, there are beginnings and endings. Is that all that "happened" means? If there is an ending, there must be a beginning, and in between is the experience. Does pointing to such units specify the truth of "happening?" How can something happen when the instant of happening is gone before you can grasp it? How can you receive a letter if the mail hasn't arrived?

The moment and the memory, the suffering and the joy—how did they arise, and where did they go when they were no longer active?

Yes, there is a story that makes sense of it, but that is only on the surface. Underneath, there is magic at work. Not a magic that discards ordinary logic, but one that makes the ordinary possible: the magic of the immediate instant. Without that magic, instant to instant, there would be no time, no transitions, no minutes, hours, or days. Yet the instant itself is openness, the unity of time.

Each day, you encounter predictable patterns and uncertainties. You experience attachment and hatred, unhappiness and dissatisfaction—the mind and senses provide the evidence needed to confirm that it is so. But who experiences, and who confirms?

Thoughts and memories, fantasies and nightmares have their own energy. If you hold on tightly to their content, you will be caught in whatever forms of suffering they impose; you will twist and turn as they tighten their hold. But what if the content does not matter? What if events are like waves in the ocean, and the time that heals them is found, not in the sequence of their occurring, but in the rhythms of their arising?

In the immediate instant, the rhythms at work do not conform to linear time. The senses offer feedback before the object manifests. Echoes reverberate before a sound is projected outward. A target is hit before the arrow is shot.

Within the Instant

Within the instant, the quality of knowing manifests differently. There are no positions, not even the position that takes no position. This is not blankness; rather, it is a kind of certainty.

For some people, the way into this certainty may be to see all appearances as paintings on water or dreams in a dreamless sleep. For others, the best way is to go into them more fully, to use them as tools for learning or vehicles for going further.

Within the instant, there is no 'to' or 'from'. There is nothing to explain. The gatekeepers, who thrive on all forms of duality, can find no footing, and the whisperer has no one to threaten or seduce. There is no 'belonging to', and there are no distractions or delusions. Ordinary time does not arise. Just as nothing separates one point of space from another a million miles away, nothing separates the immediate instant from a moment two thousand years ago, or two thousand years into the future. All points are available, equally empty and equally allowing.

Exercise 24

Being in Time

You may feel a little distanced from the instant. What is the use of such a secret inside of time, if you can't find it? But who says you aren't walking in the field of the instant all the time?

Flags move in the wind, clouds accumulate and disappear. Everything that exists appears to be traveling, journeying. Even stones are on the move; even mountains, whose shapes and forms emerge and are transformed in processes unfolding over vast periods of time.

You, too, are moving. Your heartbeat and your breath express rhythms. Your being is being in time. As you navigate time, let the instant be your lodestar.

Resting Within

To rest within the instant, it's best to let go of attachment, and suffuse your heart with compassion for all beings. Resolve to end their problems: personal problems, family problems, friend problems, national problems, global problems. Commit to ending all suffering for everyone.

"I can't!"

You can, and you must. If you don't, you are not valuing yourself, or honoring your birthright as a human being. Just say, "I will." Express your knowledge with gestures and symbols. Perhaps you don't know the gestures to use right now, but they will manifest when they are needed.

So do not be shy; let go of hesitation and pay no attention to the whispers that might lead you back into distraction. When the rigid structures of I, me, and mine begin to melt, enjoy the state of calm. Let guilt, greed, and selfishness vanish. Appreciate that the old demons of hate and desire, of pro and con, along with the solid 'reality' that experience claims, are no longer there. There is not even a 'mind' present. It is a little like learning to communicate in a different language or finding your way in the strange landscape of dream.

As you gain increasing confidence, your practice will expand in space and time. Pairs such as 'here and there', 'good and bad', will crack open like eggs, revealing their unity. You will be able to act in ordinary time, but the instant will be complete in itself.

If you try to be too clever, the words and concepts you use will stir up more patterns and more frustration. Instead, just open.

Then, open 'openness' itself.

This is not some new skill to master. Let yourself be hugged by the inner, the personal, and the genuine. Slow down and look for a quality of ease. From that relaxed place, be gentle. Teach yourself quietly.

Open all appearances, and there will be no need to ask what is happening or how it all fits together. Offering yourself hugs and kisses, you will discover the joy of being. A new certainty will prevail. Remember: you do not need special practices or esoteric teachings. Simply go within.

Open!

Expand!

A Treasure Within

Unity-Wisdom

By now, I hope you understand: There is a treasure within you, already part of your birthright. This valuable jewel is so precious and magical that when you touch it with a gesture of love, everything you wish for, everything you have been seeking for so very long, you will find is already there.

The field of mind knows this unity, which opens the character of each point of appearance to reveal inner treasures. To enter the treasure house is to embrace the heart of being.

If it's an end to suffering you want, bliss is there the moment you let go of the gatekeepers and connect to the open instant.

If you wish for inner peace, you find a fount of silent light and ease.

If it's deep understanding or knowledge you seek, wisdom beyond concepts will guide you more brightly than the light of a thousand stars.

So, what is this treasure, waiting to be awakened by your hug and kiss?

I might call it 'Great Being', or being itself, or simply unity-wisdom— an open, silent light, where knowledge, time, and space converge.

But this is ordinary language; at a deeper level, names do not apply.

No More Games

Before we encounter these teachings, when we do not yet know that a treasure like this exists, we live in a map constructed by language and mind. Like a marker on a game board, we find ourselves moving from square to square, pushed by an unseen force onto squares we did not choose.

Luck? Fate? Divine intervention? We have no way of knowing who our invisible master is, and we have no sense of control.

Landing on one square, we feel happy: someone loves us, what joy! But a short time later, we find ourselves on another square, carried there when we weren't looking by who knows what hand.

Now, what loneliness we feel! What terrible despair! Suddenly, we are imprisoned in unhappiness, with no means of escape. The next roll of the dice might bring joy again, but how can we count on that?

Pushed this way and that; exhausted by waves of emotionality; confused by the ups and downs of a mind-game whose rules we do not know and cannot fathom—surely that is no way to live!

Thank goodness, you can relax now. You have found teachings that go straight to the heart of being fully human. You no longer need to be tossed about in that old, exhausting game.

The Texture of our Lives

Please understand: What I am offering here is not a philosophy of knowledge or a psychology of action. It is not brain science, or a self-help tool designed to make you more successful, or a sociological essay on how you can best adapt to the culture we live in today.

It is not a set of instructions for entering heaven after you die, or moral advice. It is not advice at all.

What I am talking about is *how things really are* for us, and not how they seem. The very stuff that makes up the texture of our lives typically goes unexamined: the nature of self and mind, perception, cognition, language, time, the momentum toward change that makes human experience possible, in all its richness.

The message I want you to take away is this: You don't have to suffer! You can be at ease. You can find joy in whatever is happening right now, *in this instant*, in the middle of your life. There is no need for instruction, or esoteric books, or special teachers to tell you what to do. You don't have to withdraw, or escape.

Escape is a fantasy anyway, so let it go.

A Different Kind of Knowing

When we touch the silent heart of being, we release the highs and lows of thoughts and emotions; the anxious fears and the fruitless hopes; the pros and cons of confusion and ignorance that manifest daily, along with I, me, mine, and mind.

Living in the instant, at one with all that appears, we have no need or wish to shape experience or to judge it. Our actions respond to the needs that the moment presents, in the same way a parent responds to the needs of their child. The clarity, the spaciousness, the bliss that are there in the open instant eradicate frustration. Suffering finds no foothold. Love and compassion awaken, and they, in turn, transform our way of being and knowing completely.

Dwelling in the instant, we gain access to a different kind of knowing. It is not the knowing that names or senses or applies labels—not a knowing that confirms the realities of the temporal order. Rather, it is the clear light in which such ordinary knowledge is revealed. Just as light remains invisible as it moves through space, yet pervades the whole of space, so the luminosity of the instant pervades the whole of time.

In the luminosity of the instant, hate and desire, depression and confusion have no place. There is no sorting through good and bad. Borders and distinctions appear, like rainbows in the sky, but they set no limits.

The instant has no from or to, no past or future, and no present tense. The present of the instant is global, completely open. Appearance appears, but an alchemy of the instant transforms it into a global clarity and a global presence. Mind engages with ease, with no need for instructions or practices.

You can think of the instant as the 'between' that makes possible the transition from one moment to the next. We can live in that between. We can welcome it as a place of perfect wholeness and unending presence, where every action and every perception is a gesture of love.

Love Born in Freedom

Of course, 'love' is also just a word, a gesture toward what is possible. It gets used a great deal, and it can point toward all sorts of different experiences. What I am talking about is love born in freedom. Beyond words, concepts, and sensations, unimaginable, with no borders.

You do not go in search of such love, and you do not aim to teach it, not to yourself and not to others. Later, there may be interpretations and explanations, but the truth of love comes before all that.

Instant to instant, the very qualities that lead to suffering—attachment, grasping, emotionality, confusion—offer the seeds of perfect union. In such union, there are no units and no territories. There is no friction. Beginning is the same as ending, and one is not different from zero. The zero that we know, that we inscribe on paper or use in our calculations, is a symbol of such possibilities, a point that points equally toward the past instant and future instant, the ending instant and the beginning instant.

We know quite well how to establish separate points and identities, how to act in time and manifest in space. Now we need to discover the unity of all such distinctions. We need to recognize that whether we go to the source of the river or the mouth of the river, the water remains the same.

Connecting to the Heart of Being

So, there it is. Complex, yes.

But simple, as well.

Hugging and kissing, embracing the silent field of being, we are no longer stuck. We can draw on experiences from the past and plan for the future—ordinary happenings in linear time—and we can also dwell within the infinitesimal instant, where time has no dimensions.

We can meet deadlines, celebrate birthdays and weddings, and also know that we are part of a long lineage reaching back to the stars, and stretching forward into a limitless future. There is no need to choose.

We can model ourselves on the great spiritual beings who once walked on earth, letting goodness, kindness, and transcendent knowledge become our way of being. The same qualities they displayed are still available, right now. Why not expand them? Why not embody love and limitless caring? The world needs this very badly!

We can follow in the footsteps of the many inspiring people who have contributed to our culture and shaped our bodies of knowledge. We can kiss the depths of open being, and choose also to be engaged in the everyday world around us. We can use language to guide people and share with them what we know, while also understanding the limitations of concepts and words.

We can offer hugs and kisses to all beings who have ever lived throughout time and space, sharing with them our new-found joy and inner peace. And we can focus our energy on supporting whatever we care about—justice for all; remedies for climate change; world peace; gardening; animal rights, creating art, or simply taking care of ourselves and our loved ones.

Being is not an abstraction. From its depth, creativity, generosity, selflessness, joy, wisdom, peace, and love are born. When we embody these qualities, we think, love, live, and breathe in new ways. Loneliness, anger, and envy fall away. We let go of the gatekeepers and give up our identity cards.

We and whatever appears are no longer divided, so pros and cons cannot confuse us. Time, space, and knowledge are unified, yet we can draw freely from each of them. In the open field at the heart of being, all of our potential as human beings can unfold.

Instructions Aren't Necessary

Do you see now? There is nothing missing! There is nothing you need to have, and nothing you need to do *before* you can let go of suffering. Instructions aren't necessary; you already know the benefit of hugs and kisses, and you can follow the path of your own inner knowing.

Gateways aren't necessary, either. There are no walls in an open field to serve as barriers, so, where would you place a gate?

The instant may be the smallest moment there is, but from another perspective it is also vast; it contains all the angles of time. You can operate as though the past and the future are real, but in fact you are never apart from the immediacy of the instant.

So, you don't have to struggle to scrunch your way into a tiny unit of time. The instant doesn't have units, and there are no boundaries between instants. Without units or boundaries, concepts like 'in' and 'out' or 'between' simply do not apply.

Wherever you are is the instant, and the instant is always the right time to be!

You Never Need to Be Fooled Again

So, let go of "I can't," or "I don't know how." Bring ease to whatever arises, all of the dream-like bubbles.

Smile. Enjoy the display!

Thoughts, emotions, perceptions, and sensations, are merely appearances. They come and go like dreams. The only thing that makes them seem real is the regime's magic, which partners with ignorance to create an illusion: the illusion of *I am*, the illusion of *it is*, the illusion of *from* and *to*, of linear time, and of the identity structures that create suffering.

Stop looking for signs of progress or positive experiences. Those are all just ideas. If you set out to find a road or path, the very efforts you make will become an obstacle: nothing more than fixations and frictions. Let go of all that. Freedom from the regime of mind comes from within, and it is already available. So relax. Even the possibility of freedom can become an obstacle if you hold on to it tightly.

You never need to be fooled again. When appearances arise, no matter what their shape or content, you don't need to push them away, and you don't need to engage them. Now you know them for what they are. You can embrace them, kiss them, and let them dissolve because you know they are inherently insubstantial. The nature of dreams is to disappear.

Perhaps you have moments when this imperfectly expressed possibility makes sense. When they come, let them expand, and you will find that you are very close to what we might call 'being'.

So, give yourself hugs and kisses, and let joy and love expand.

Silent light is already shining.

The Great Love at the heart of being is already here!

List of Exercises

A Life Devoted to Dharma Activity

Tarthang Tulku, also known as Kunga Gellek Yeshe Dorje, was born in Golok, Eastern Tibet, in 1935. He is one of the last surviving Tibetan lamas to receive a comprehensive traditional education in Old Tibet.

As a young tulku, he studied intensively with more than twenty celebrated masters, traveling widely throughout Eastern Tibet. His root guru was Jamyang Khyentse Chokyi Lodro, one of the most remarkable Tibetan masters of the twentieth century. In 1958, Tarthang Tulku followed this master on a journey to Sikkim, just escaping the annexation of his country by the Chinese. At the young age of 23, he became a refugee in India.

After a short stay at the Young Lamas Home School in Dalhousie, he was asked by H.H. Dudjom Rinpoche to represent the Nyingma school at Sanskrit University in Varanasi. There he established Dharma Mudranalaya to print Tibetan Buddhist texts. In 1968 he left India for the United States, becoming the first Nyingma lama in America.

In 1969, Rinpoche founded the Tibetan Nyingma Meditation Center (TNMC), a California corporation sole, as the nucleus of his activities. He established Padma Ling as the residential headquarters of TNMC, and in 1972-73 founded the Nyingma Institute, where he taught publicly until 1978. During these years, he published the first of his nearly three dozen original books in English. He also founded the Tibetan Aid Project to support Tibetans in exile; Dharma Press and Dharma Publishing, which have now printed and reproduced hundreds of art reproductions and more than 288 books for Western students, translated into 18 languages; Nyingma Centers, to guide the growth of four international centers, in Amsterdam, Köln, São Paulo and Rio de Janeiro, with a new center, as of 2020, emerging in Porto Allegre; and Odiyan Retreat Center, a mandala of temples, stupas, and libraries, including Vajra Temple, Cintamani Temple, the Enlightenment Stupa, and Vairocana Garden. Consecrated in 2019, Odiyan's Dharma Wheel Mandala surrounds the Mandala's central temple complex with 2,016 18-inch-tall Prayer Wheels, each of which contains all the texts of the Kanjur; it is the largest monument of its kind in the world.

Ratna Ling Retreat Center, established in 2004 as an adjunct to Odiyan, offers retreats to the general public on topics that encourage the integration of mind and body and emphasize many forms of wellness. A special facility to house and support elder members of the TNMC community is in development.

In 1981 Rinpoche published the *Nyingma Edition of the Tibetan Buddhist Canon* in 120 atlas-sized volumes, followed by an eight-volume Catalogue and Bibliography. The Yeshe De Text Project, founded in 1983, produced *Great Treasures of Ancient Teachings* in 637 volumes, and has printed and distributed to the Tibetan community an enormous treasure of sacred books, including six editions of the Kanjur and three of the Tanjur. Its most recent edition, the *Yid bzhin Norbu Kanjur*, may be the most comprehensive Kanjur collection ever

assembled. In all, more than 10,000 sets of the Kanjur have been offered to the Tibetan Sangha.

In 1989 Rinpoche founded the Nyingma Monlam Chenmo (World Peace Ceremony) in Bodh Gaya, India, where 8,000-10,000 monastics and lay faithful gather annually. He also provided seed money to the other major schools of Tibetan Buddhism for Kagyu, Sakya, and Gelug Monlams. Through the Monlam, Rinpoche was able to make extraordinary text offerings to the Sangha. Yeshe De's recent offerings include collected works of great masters like Jigme Lingpa, Patrul Rinpoche and Lama Mipham. As many as 100 unique volumes of texts can be offered in a given year, with thousands of copies of each volume being provided free of charge to the libraries of Dharma centers throughout the Tibetan diaspora. A participant who received books every year of the Monlam would now have a personal Yeshe De library consisting of more than a thousand volumes. Since 1989, along with more than five million sacred books, TNMC has distributed 3.25 million sacred art images and 176,250 prayer wheels to more than 3,300 Dharma centers in India, Nepal, Bhutan, and Tibet. Thousands of bronze reproductions of authentic ancient sacred images created at Odiyan have also been offered to the Sangha. A total of 92,694 copies of the precious 8,000-line Prajnaparamita—including 414 granite plaques engraved in Sanskrit, Tibetan, and English, 10 large hand-sewn victory banners, and six important editions in Traditional Tibetan format—have been offered to the Sangha.

Other offerings for Bodh Gaya include eight butterlamp houses; hundreds of prayer wheels; golden lantsa and Tibetan Prajnaparamita plaques; financial support for the restoration of the Mahabodhi Temple spire; site beautification; fabric banners, hangings, and umbrellas produced at Odiyan; and year-round offerings of butterlamps.

In 2002, to support the restoration of Buddhism in the land of its origin, Rinpoche founded the Light of Buddhadharma Foundation International (LBDFI). In 2006, TNMC and LBDFI jointly sponsored and organized the first annual Tipitaka Chanting Ceremony by the Theravadin Sangha in Bodh Gaya—the first gathering of its kind in more than 700 years.

As this annual ceremony continues to be held, additional Tipitaka Chanting Ceremonies are being organized and held around the world, including Berkeley, CA; representatives from eleven countries now participate. LBDFI's work has been embraced by the Indian government, which enthusiastically supports initiatives like the Dharma Training Wheel, bringing venerable monks on an extended pilgrimage to the Eight Great Holy Places of the Buddha.

TNMC and its mandala organizations have installed seventeen 2½-ton World Peace Bells at holy places throughout Asia, and have supported renovation projects at numerous sacred sites, including the historic renovation of the Swayambhu Stupa in Nepal. Other major restoration projects include the refounding of the practice center of the great twentieth

century renunciate master Khenpo Chokyab, and the restoration of Adzom Gar, the seat of Adzom Drukpa and Rinpoche's own teacher, Adzom Drukpa's son and heir A-'gyur Rinpoche.

In 2005, Mangalam Light Foundation was established. Operating through four 'daughter' foundations, with LBDFI being joined by the Ananda, Prajna, and Vajra Light Foundations, Mangalam Light's mission is to revive, preserve, and support the heritage of the Buddhadharma in Tibet. The Tibet-based Light Foundations have given substantial support to many diverse projects, including construction at Tarthang Monastery in Eastern Tibet. Ananda Light Foundation has funded repairs and construction at numerous monasteries and nunneries; it has also built primary schools serving 800 children throughout Eastern Tibet. Vajra Light Foundation has provided ceremony support throughout Central and Eastern Tibet, particularly sponsoring large Monlams at Larung Gar and Yachen Gar, respectively the largest Buddhist monastery in the world and the largest nunnery in Tibet. Prajna Light Foundation has made great efforts to restore Tibetan libraries: more than 1,000 sets of the Kanjur and 10,000 sets of the collected works of the great Nyingma master Longchenpa have been distributed to monasteries throughout Tibet.

In 2009, Rinpoche founded the Mangalam Research Center for Buddhist Languages in Berkeley, CA. Partnering with a distinguished group of international scholars, MRC has received several prestigious grants from the National Endowment for the Humanities, enabling it to develop the highly innovative Buddhist Translators' Workbench data tool for researchers. It also offers many conferences, colloquia and seminars, as well as numerous programs open to the public. In the same period, Rinpoche founded Guna Foundation, a documentary filmmaking unit that has produced three well-received documentaries on Tarthang Tulku's Dharma activities, including the award-winning film, *The Great Transmission* (2016).

In 2012, Rinpoche established Dharma College in downtown Berkeley to serve as a site for the exploration of dynamic and synergistic new teachings on the nature of the mind, expressed in recent books like *Revelations of Mind, Dimensions of Mind, Keys of Knowledge,* and the *Lotus Trilogy.* 2013 saw the inauguration of Sarnath International Nyingma Institute (SINI) in Sarnath, India, founded by Rinpoche in order to bridge the gap between Eastern and Western modes of knowledge, to foster the study of the earliest period of Tibetan Buddhism (embodied in Khen Lob Cho Sum, the Founders of Tibetan Dharma), and to host the annual Tibet Peace Ceremony. SINI is also home to the ecumenical Kanjur Karchag Project, which gathers Tibetan scholars from all major schools in a deep study of the origins and structure of the Tibetan Kanjur. As the TNMC mandala continues to unfold, the Nyingma Association of Mandala Organizations (NAMO), incorporated in 2012, helps guide and protect the work of its seventeen distinct member organizations.

In 2018, Rinpoche published *Caring,* an accessible exploration of the power of compassion in healing ourselves and the world around us. New programs based on *Caring* are being offered throughout the TNMC mandala. As of 2022, online programs for the public on a wide variety of topics are available from the Nyingma Institute, Dharma College, Ratna Ling, Odiyan, and the international centers.

Rinpoche has dedicated his life to the work of preserving, protecting and distributing the Tibetan Buddhist heritage. All his books and projects are efforts to manifest the sacred forms of Kaya, Vaca, Citta, Guna, and Karma—enlightened embodiment speech, mind, qualities, and actions—for the sake of the entire world. More information about these activities is recorded in more than 45 volumes of the TNMC Annals, copies of which can be found at the Nyingma Institute and the international centers. Now in his mid-eighties, Rinpoche continues to preserve and distribute sacred Tibetan texts, to write books for Western audiences, and to energetically direct large, innovative and inspiring Dharma projects.

About Dharma Publishing

Dharma Publishing, established in the US in 1969, has produced more than 288 titles in English that introduce fundamental Dharma concepts, Buddhist history, art and culture, and more than 45 original works by Tarthang Tulku.

Tarthang Tulku has created innovative teachings for modern readers that integrate psychology and meditation, forming a bridge between traditional philosophy and secular inquiry of the human mind. His penetrating insights into the workings of the mind have been cherished by generations of academic and lay audiences.

At the core of his teachings and work is a deep appreciation of human potential, and the transformative power of the mind.

Tarthang Tulku continues to work, writing books, leading large-scale cultural preservation projects, and devoting his days to prayer, contemplation, and the spiritual guidance of his community.

In *Gesture of Great Love*, themes from earlier books by Tarthang Tulku come together and meet, right in the human heart.

If you enjoyed reading *Gesture of Great Love*,
you may also enjoy the titles below:

Gesture of Balance
Time, Space, and Knowledge
Hidden Mind of Freedom
Dynamics of Time and Space
Revelations of Mind
Caring

To explore other Dharma Publishing books,
visit www.dharmapublishing.com

To support readers' understanding, the Dharma Publishing
Academy offers a remarkable resource for online study
of the teachings of Tarthang Tulku:
www.academy.dharmapublishing.com

For online programs and in-person classes and retreats
based on Dharma Publishing books,
visit these organizations founded by Tarthang Tulku

Centers in the United States

Nyingma Institute: www.nyingmainstitute.com
Dharma College: www.dharma-college.com
Mangalam Research Center: www.mangalamresearch.org
Center for Creative Inquiry: www.creativeinquiry.org
Ratna Ling Retreat Center: www.ratnaling.org
Odiyan Retreat Center: www.odiyan.org

International Centers

Amsterdam, Holland: www.nyingma.nl
Cologne, Germany: www.nyingmazentrum.de
Sao Paulo, Brazil: www.centronyingmabrasil.org
Rio de Janeiro, Brazil: www.nyingmario.org.br
Porto Alegre, Brazil: www.nyingmapoa.org.br
Nyingma Group Israel: www.nyingmaisrael.org
Buenos Aires, Argentina: Argentina Kum Nye group